FIRST STEP IN KOREAN

외국인을 위한

한국어 입문

Compiled by
The Institute of Continuing Education
of Kyung Hee University

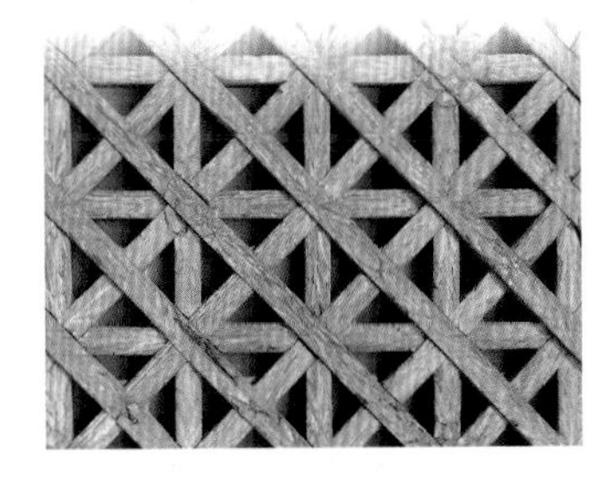

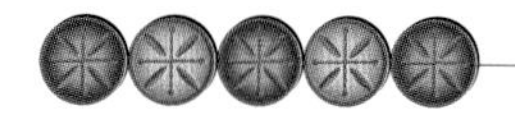

- **Suk-Ja Lee**
  Professor of the Department of Japanese Language and Literature at Kyung Hee University
- **Hyran Lee**
  Head Professor of the Foreign Language Program of ICE at Kyung Hee University
- **Suk-Man Lee**
  Missionary of the Baptist Church
- **Choon-Seung Kim**
  Former Lecturer of Korean Language Program of ICE at Kyung Hee University
- **Steven Song**
  Lecturer of the English Program of ICE at Kyung Hee University
- **Jung-Sik Jung**
  High School Teacher for the Japanese Language Classes
- **Yo-Hui Lee**
  Lecturer of the Japanese Language and Literature at Kyung Hee University
- **Jae-Heon Lee**
  MA in the Japanese Language and Literature at Kyung Hee University / Provided illustrations for this book

FIRST STEP IN KOREAN

Published by MINJUNG SEORIM
37-29, Hoedong-gil, Paju-si,
Gyeonggi-do 413-120, KOREA
Phone: (031) 955-6500~6 Fax: (031) 955-6525~6

Price: 13,000 Won
ISBN: 978-89-387-0041-1 13710

Printed in Korea

■ Traditional Roofs with Tiles

■ Panoramic view of Seoul

■ Taegwondo

한국의 전통 문화 Ⅱ

KOREAN TRADITIONAL CULTURE(Ⅱ)

남대문
namdaemun
Namdaemun: South Palace Gate

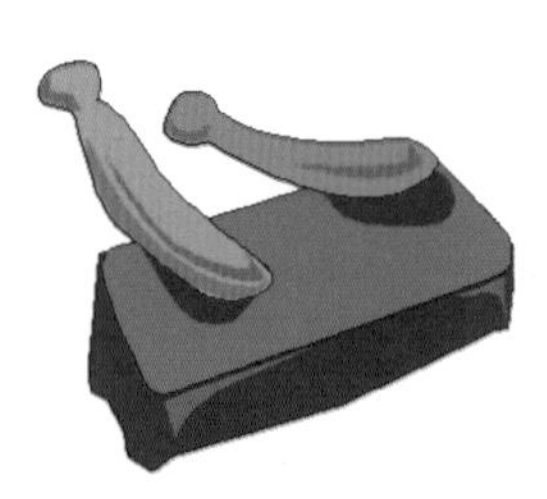

다듬이
dadeumi
Traditional Tool Used for Straightening Clothes

탑
tap
Pagoda

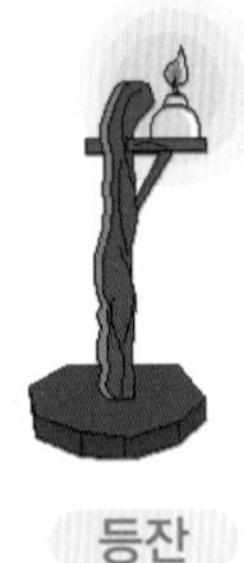

등잔
deungjan
Traditional Oil Lamp

떡
tteok
Rice Cake

맷돌
maetdol
Traditional Stone Grinder

화로
hwaro
Traditional Fire Pot

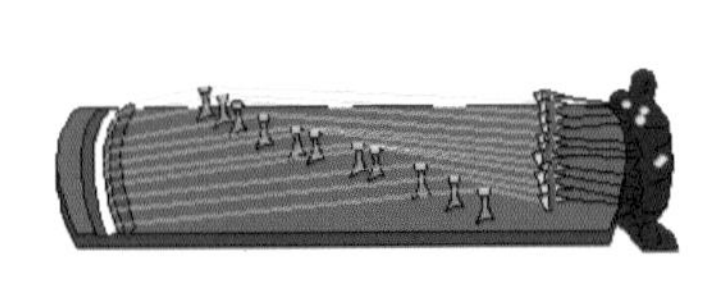

가야금
gayageum
Traditional Stringed Instrument

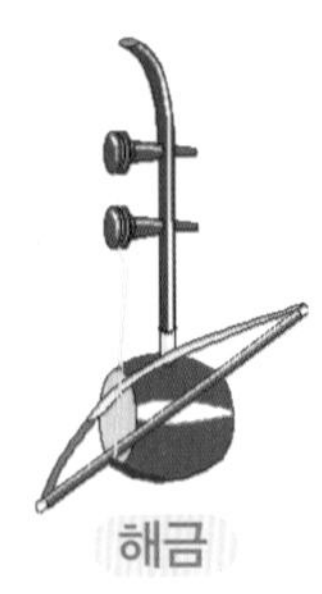

해금
haegeum
Traditional Stringed Instrument

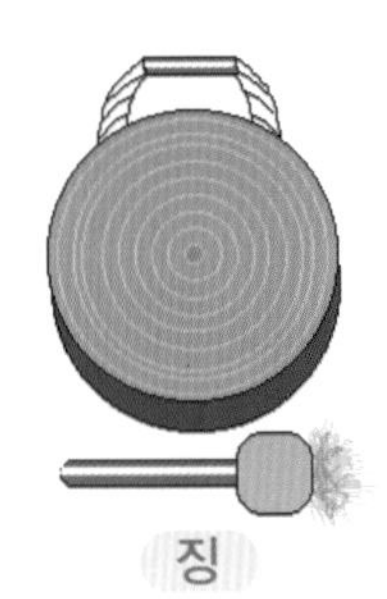

징
jing
Traditional Gong

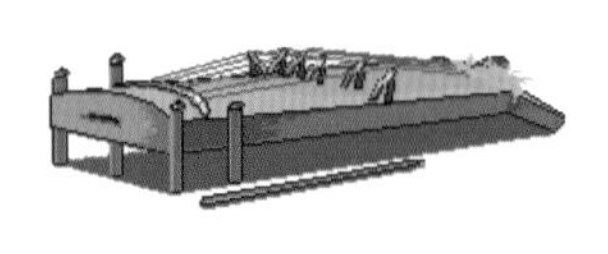

아쟁
ajaeng
Traditional Stringed Instrument

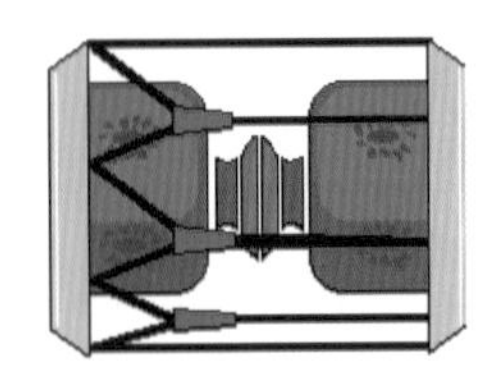

장구
jang-gu
Traditional Drum

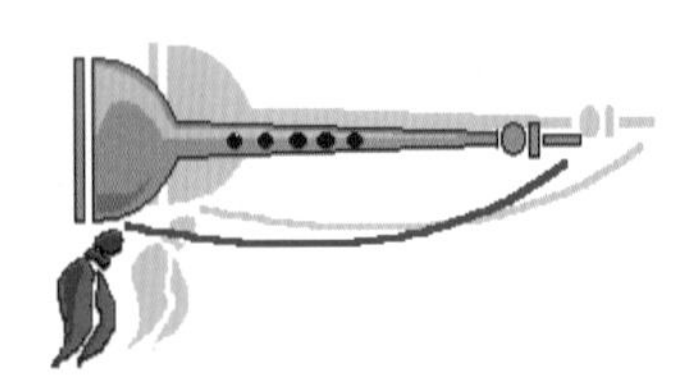

태평소
taepyeongso
Traditional Horn

피리
piri
Traditional Flute

한국의 전통 문화 I
KOREAN TRADITIONAL CULTURE(I)

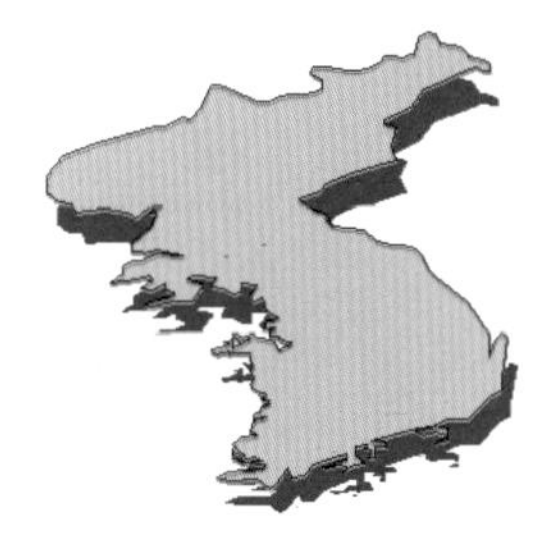
한국 지도
hanguk jido
Map of Korea

태극기
taegeuk-gi
National Flag

널뛰기
neolttwigi
Traditional See-Saw

댕기머리
daenggimeori
Traditional Braided Hair Style

부채춤
buchaechum
Traditional Fan Dance

스님
seunim
Buddhist Monk

상모돌리기
sangmodolligi
Traditional Dance Using a Ribbon Attached to a Hat

신부
sinbu
Bride

살풀이춤
salpurichum
Traditional Dance Comforting a Spirit

가마
gama
Palanquin (Traditional Hand Carriage)

갓
gat
Traditional Hat

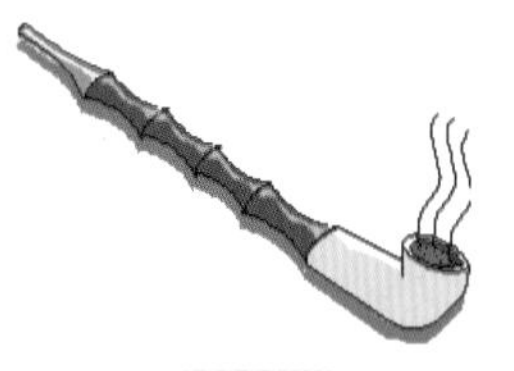
곰방대
gombangdae
Smoking Pipe

3 Syllable Final Consonant Clusters (받침)

consonants	pronunciation	order of formation	writing practice			
ㄱ	-k	ㄱ, ㅋ, ㄳ, ㄺ, ㄲ	학교 hakgyo school		닭 dak chicken	
ㄴ	-n	ㄴ, ㄵ, ㄶ	전화 jeonhwa telephone		많다 manta many	
ㄷ	-t	ㄷ, ㅅ, ㅆ, ㅈ, ㅊ, ㅌ, ㅎ	옷 ot clothes		빛 bit light	
ㄹ	-l	ㄹ, ㄼ, ㄾ, ㅀ, ㄺ, ㄳ	얼굴 eolgul face		여덟 yeodeol eight	
ㅁ	-m	ㅁ, ㄻ	담배 dambae cigarette		젊다 jeomda to be young	
ㅂ	-p	ㅂ, ㅍ, ㅄ, ㄼ, ㄿ	접시 jeopsi dish	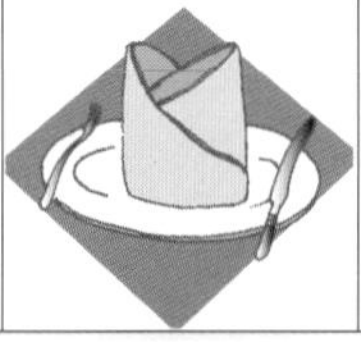	잎 ip leaf	
ㅇ	-ng	ㅇ	종 jong bell		병아리 byeong-ari chick	

consonants	pronunciation	order of formation	writing practice				
ㄲ	kk [ssanggiyeok]	ㄲ	ㄲ ㄲ	ㄲ ㄲ		꽃 kkot flower	
ㄸ	tt [ssangdigeut]	ㄸ	ㄸ ㄸ	ㄸ ㄸ		뚱보 ttungbo fat person	
ㅃ	pp [ssangbieup]	ㅃ	ㅃ ㅃ	ㅃ ㅃ		빵 ppang bread	
ㅆ	ss [ssangsiot]	ㅆ	ㅆ ㅆ	ㅆ ㅆ		싸움 ssaum quarrel	
ㅉ	jj [ssangjieut]	ㅉ	ㅉ ㅉ	ㅉ ㅉ		쪽지 jjokji a slip of paper	

consonants	pronunciation	order of formation	writing practice				
ㅇ	ø, ng [ieung]	ㅇ (1)	ㅇ ㅇ	ㅇ ㅇ		아기 agi baby	
ㅈ	j [jieut]	ㅈ (1, 2)	ㅈ ㅈ	ㅈ ㅈ		장미 jangmi rose	
ㅊ	ch [chieut]	ㅊ (1, 2, 3)	ㅊ ㅊ	ㅊ ㅊ		책 chaek book	
ㅋ	k [kieuk]	ㅋ (1, 2)	ㅋ ㅋ	ㅋ ㅋ		코 ko nose	
ㅌ	t [tieut]	ㅌ (1, 2, 3)	ㅌ ㅌ	ㅌ ㅌ		탑 tap pagoda	
ㅍ	p [pieup]	ㅍ (1, 2, 3, 4)	ㅍ ㅍ	ㅍ ㅍ		팔 pal arm	
ㅎ	h [hieut]	ㅎ (1, 2, 3)	ㅎ ㅎ	ㅎ ㅎ		하늘 haneul sky	

제 1 과
Lesson 1

안녕하세요? Hi.

Key Sentences

1. 안녕하세요? — Hi.
   annyeonghaseyo
2. 당신은 어느 나라 사람입니까? — Which country are you from?
   dangsineun eoneu nara saramimnikka

Dialogs

Dialog 1

수미: 안녕하세요? Hi.
annyeonghaseyo

헨리: 안녕하세요? Hi.
annyeonghaseyo

수미: 이름이 무엇입니까?
ireumi mueosimnikka
What's your name?

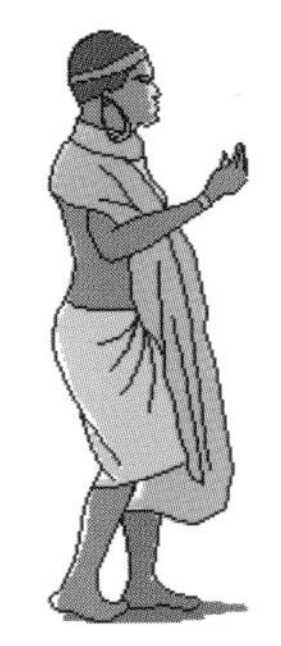

헨리: 헨리입니다. My name is Henry.
henriimnida

당신의 이름은 무엇이에요? What's your name?
dangsinui ireumeun mueosieyo

수미: 제 이름은 이수미입니다. My name is Lee, Sumi.
je ireumeun isumiimnida

만나서 반갑습니다. It's nice to meet you.
mannaseo bangapseumnida

헨리: 만나서 반갑습니다. It's nice to meet you.
mannaseo bangapseumnida

Dialog 2

수미: 당신은 어느 나라 사람입니까? Which country are you from?
dangsineun eoneu nara saramimnikka

헨리: 저는 나이지리아 사람입니다.
jeoneun naijiria saramimnida
I'm a Nigerian.

수미: 당신도 나이지리아 사람입니까?
dangsindo naijiria saramimnikka
Are you also a Nigerian?

존슨: 아니오, 나이지리아 사람이 아닙니다.
anio naijiria sarami animnida
No, I'm not from Nigeria.

저는 미얀마 사람입니다.
jeoneun miyanma saramimnida
I'm from Myanmar.

Vocabulary and Phrases

- 안녕하세요? hello
- 무엇입니까? What is(are)…?
- 이름 name
- 당신, 너 you
- 이다 to be
- 미얀마 Myanmar
- 어느 which
- 나이지리아 Nigeria
- 아니오 no
- 아니다 not
- 반갑습니다 to be nice to
- 저, 나 I
- 만나다 to meet
- 사람 people
- 나라 country

Word Drills

미국 [miguk] U.S.A.		나이지리아 [naijiria] Nigeria	
일본 [ilbon] Japan		미얀마 [miyanma] Myanmar	
중국 [jungguk] China		파키스탄 [pakistan] Pakistan	
호주 [hoju] Australia		한국 [hanguk] Korea	

2 Consonants (한글의 기본 자음)

consonants	pronunciation	order of formation	writing practice				
ㄱ	g, k [giyeok]	ㄱ	ㄱ ㄱ	ㄱ ㄱ		가위 gawi scissors	
ㄴ	n [nieun]	ㄴ	ㄴ ㄴ	ㄴ ㄴ		나비 nabi butterfly	
ㄷ	d, t [digeut]	ㄷ	ㄷ ㄷ	ㄷ ㄷ		도로 doro road	
ㄹ	r, l [rieul]	ㄹ	ㄹ ㄹ	ㄹ ㄹ		로켓 roket rocket	
ㅁ	m [mieum]	ㅁ	ㅁ ㅁ	ㅁ ㅁ		말 mal horse	
ㅂ	b, p [bieup]	ㅂ	ㅂ ㅂ	ㅂ ㅂ		바지 baji trousers	
ㅅ	s [siot]	ㅅ	ㅅ ㅅ	ㅅ ㅅ		사과 sagwa apple	

vowels	pronunciation	order of formation	writing practice				
ㅘ	wa 와	ㅘ 1 2 3 4	ㅘ ㅘ	ㅘ ㅘ		과일 gwail fruit	
ㅙ	wae 왜	ㅙ 1 2 3 4 5	ㅙ ㅙ	ㅙ ㅙ		돼지 dwaeji pig	
ㅚ	oe 외	ㅚ 1 2 3	ㅚ ㅚ	ㅚ ㅚ		왼쪽 oenjjok left side	
ㅝ	wo 워	ㅝ 1 2 3 4	ㅝ ㅝ	ㅝ ㅝ		원숭이 wonsung-i monkey	
ㅞ	we 웨	ㅞ 1 2 3 4 5	ㅞ ㅞ	ㅞ ㅞ		웨이터 weiteo waiter	
ㅟ	wi 위	ㅟ 1 2 3	ㅟ ㅟ	ㅟ ㅟ		귀 gwi ear	
ㅢ	ui 의	ㅢ 1 2	ㅢ ㅢ	ㅢ ㅢ		의사 uisa doctor	

vowels	pronunciation	order of formation	writing practice				
ㅠ	yu 유	ㅠ	ㅠ ㅠ	ㅠ ㅠ		귤 gyul orange	
ㅡ	eu 으	ㅡ	ㅡ ㅡ	ㅡ ㅡ		트럭 teureok truck	
ㅣ	i 이	ㅣ	ㅣ ㅣ	ㅣ ㅣ		기차 gicha train	
ㅐ	ae 애	ㅐ	ㅐ ㅐ	ㅐ ㅐ		개구리 gaeguri frog	
ㅒ	yae 얘	ㅒ	ㅒ ㅒ	ㅒ ㅒ		얘 yae this child	
ㅔ	e 에	ㅔ	ㅔ ㅔ	ㅔ ㅔ		게 ge crab	
ㅖ	ye 예	ㅖ	ㅖ ㅖ	ㅖ ㅖ		계단 gyedan stairway	

Korean Vowels and Consonants

❶ Vowels (한글의 기본 모음)

vowels	pronunciation	order of formation	writing practice				
ㅏ	a 아	ㅏ 1 2	ㅏ ㅏ ㅏ ㅏ			사자 saja lion	
ㅑ	ya 야	ㅑ 1 2 3	ㅑ ㅑ ㅑ ㅑ			야구 yagu baseball	
ㅓ	eo 어	ㅓ 1 2	ㅓ ㅓ ㅓ ㅓ			머리 meori head	
ㅕ	yeo 여	ㅕ 1 2 3	ㅕ ㅕ ㅕ ㅕ			별 byeol star	
ㅗ	o 오	ㅗ 1 2	ㅗ ㅗ ㅗ ㅗ			모자 moja cap	
ㅛ	yo 요	ㅛ 1 2 3	ㅛ ㅛ ㅛ ㅛ			교회 gyohwoe church	
ㅜ	u 우	ㅜ 1 2	ㅜ ㅜ ㅜ ㅜ			우유 uyu milk	

PART III

제 14 과
je sipsagwa
Lesson 14

은행에서
eunhaengeseo
At the Bank 79

제 15 과
je sibogwa
Lesson 15

백화점에서
baekwhajeomeseo
At the Department Store 85

제 16 과
je simyukgwa
Lesson 16

편지 쓰기
pyeonjisseugi
Writing a Letter 91

제 17 과
je sipchilgwa
Lesson 17

어디가 아프십니까?
eodiga apeushimnikka
Where Does It Hurt? 97

제 18 과
je sippalgwa
Lesson 18

무슨 운동을 좋아하십니까?
museun undong-eul joahasimnikka
What Sports Do You Like? 103

제 19 과
je sipgugwa
Lesson 19

세탁물을 맡기려고 합니다.
setakmureul matgiryeogo hamnida
I'm Going to Have My Laundry Drycleaned. 109

제 20 과
je isipgwa
Lesson 20

편지를 쓰고 있습니다.
pyeonjireul sseugo itseumnida
I'm Writing a Letter. 115

Map of Korea 122

Index 123

제 6 과 je yukgwa Lesson 6
생일이 언제예요?
saeng-iri eonjeyeyo
When Is Your Birthday? 31

PART II

제 7 과 je chilgwa Lesson 7
몇 개 있어요?
myeot gae isseoyo
How Many Do You Have? 37

제 8 과 je palgwa Lesson 8
얼마입니까?
eolmaimnikka
How Much Is It? 43

제 9 과 je gugwa Lesson 9
비빔밥 한 그릇 주세요.
bibimbap han geureut juseyo
Please Give Me One Bibimbap. 49

제 10 과 je sipgwa Lesson 10
여보세요?
yeoboseyo
Hello? 55

제 11 과 je sibilgwa Lesson 11
이태원은 어떻게 가요?
itaewoneun eotteoke gayo
How Do I Get to Itaewon? 61

제 12 과 je sibigwa Lesson 12
저는 내일 여행 갈 거예요.
joeneun naeil yeohaeng gal geoyeyo
I'm Going on a Trip Tomorrow. 67

제 13 과 je sipsamgwa Lesson 13
방 구하기
bang guhagi
Renting a House 73

CONTENTS

머리말
meorimal
Preface iii

일러두기
ilreodugi
Introduction
Abbreviation of Symbols
Korean Pronunciation iv

한글의 기본 모음 · 자음
hangeurui gibon moeum · jaeum
Korean Vowels and Consonants xi
한국의 전통 문화 (I, II)

PART I

제1과
je ilgwa
Lesson 1
안녕하세요?
annyeonghaseyo
Hi. 1

제2과
je igwa
Lesson 2
아버지의 직업은 무엇입니까?
abeojiui jigeobeun mueosimnikka
What's Your Father's Occupation? 7

제3과
je samgwa
Lesson 3
어디 있어요?
eodi isseoyo
Where Is It? 13

제4과
je sagwa
Lesson 4
이것은 한국어로 무엇입니까?
igeoseun hangugeoro mueosimnikka
What Is This in Korean? 19

제5과
je ogwa
Lesson 5
어느 계절을 좋아해요?
eoneu gyejeoreul joahaeyo
Which Season Do You Like? 25

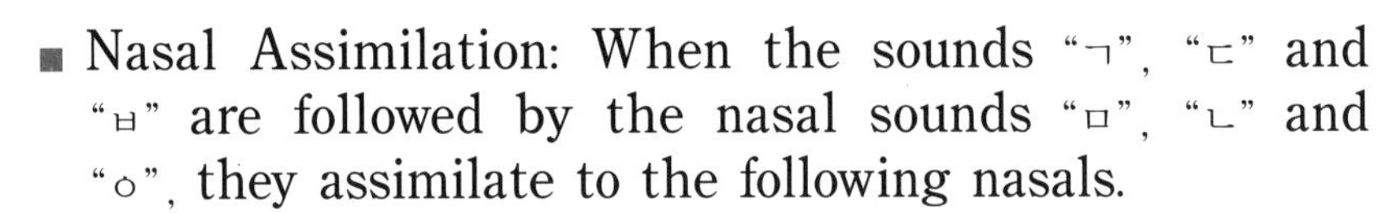

■ Nasal Assimilation: When the sounds “ㄱ”, “ㄷ” and “ㅂ” are followed by the nasal sounds “ㅁ”, “ㄴ” and “ㅇ”, they assimilate to the following nasals.

Ex) 낱말 [난말] words　　　작년 [장년] last year

■ Palatalization: The syllable final consonants “ㄷ” and “ㅌ” are pronounced as “ㅈ” or “ㅊ” when followed by the vowel “이”.

Ex) 맏이 [마지] first son(daughter)
　　 같이 [가치] together

■ Lateralization : “ㄴ” is pronounced as “ㄹ” before or after “ㄹ”

Ex) 천리 [철리] 1000 ri
　　 달나라 [달라라] moon land

■ Aspiration: The consonants are aspirated after the sound “ㅎ”.

Ex) 좋다 [조타] to be good　　　많다 [만타] many

■ Vowel contraction: The sequence of vowels can be contracted.

Ex)

오 [o] + 아 [a] → 와 [wa]	우 [u] + 어 [eo] → 워 [wo]
이 [i] + 아 [a] → 야 [ya]	이 [i] + 어 [eo] → 여 [yeo]
이 [i] + 오 [o] → 요 [yo]	이 [i] + 우 [u] → 유 [yu]
아 [a] + 이 [i] → 애 [ae]	

Abbreviation of Symbols

( ) means either optional choice or a root form of a verb.
→ means 'changes to' or 'becomes'.
\+ indicates a boundary of morphemes.
– indicates a bound form.

Korean Pronunciation

- Syllable Final Neutralization: Consonants such as "ㄷ", "ㅌ", "ㅈ", "ㅊ", "ㅅ", and "ㅆ" are pronounced as an unreleased "ㄷ" in the syllable final position. Consonants such as "ㄱ", "ㄲ" and "ㅋ" are pronounced as an unreleased "ㄱ" in the syllable final position. Consonants such as "ㅂ" and "ㅍ" are pronounced as an unreleased "ㅂ" in the same position.

  Ex) 밭 [받] field　　빛 [빋] light
  부엌 [부억] kitchen　　앞 [압] front

- Consonant-to-Vowel Linking: When followed by a vowel, the syllable final consonant is pronounced in the initial position of the following vowel.

  Ex) 한국어 [한구거] the Korean language
  묻어 [무더] to stain　　직업 [지겁] occupation
  월요일 [워료일] Monday

- Tensification: The consonants "ㄱ", "ㄷ", "ㅂ", "ㅅ" and "ㅈ" become the tense consonants "ㄲ", "ㄸ", "ㅃ", "ㅆ", and "ㅉ" when followed by any consonants except "ㄴ", "ㄹ", "ㅁ", "ㅇ" and "ㅎ".

  Ex) 학교 [학꾜] school　　닫다 [닫따] to close
  맛보다 [맏뽀다] to taste　　젖다 [젇따] get wet

Because this book is designed for foreigners at the beginning level, romanization which is done by the Ministry of Education is given throughout all lessons along with English translation. However, romanization should be used at a minimum only to confirm one's pronunciation when necessary. The Korean language is based on the sound system like English, so if one learns the sound system in the beginning section, one won't need to use romanization. For English translation, Korean and English cannot make a one-to-one correspondence in structures and words. English translation helps the student understand the meaning of the Korean sentences. Hence it should be used to grasp the meaning of the whole sentence, not each word or a part of a structure. At any rate, romanization and English translation could help one access to the Korean language at the beginning level more easily.

For reference, an index is provided at the back of the text. When one has a question about a word or expression, or grammar, one can refer to the index section. Apart from English, Chinese and Japanese translations are given for the readers from those language groups who have some difficulties in learning by means of English.

The basic Chinese characters are also attached at the back. The Korean language uses many Chinese characters. Anyone who wants to learn Korean should know the basic Chinese characters, which are essential to increase one's vocabulary. Chinese characters are especially needed to those people who want to take the "Korean Competency Test".

The Korean way of mcasuring, wcighing, and counting is attached in a table, compared to the English units of measuring. To settle in a new environment, one needs to refer to this page frequently.

In an overall view, this book is organized into three parts of 20 lessons; the first part with 6 lessons, the second part with 7 lessons, and the third part with 7 lessons. Each lesson consists of Vocabulary and Phrases, Word Drills, Structures and Expressions, Exercises and Reading Practice. At the beginning the Hangeul letters are introduced, and at the back in the appendix, the index, measuring units, and basic Chinese characters are attached. If one studies this book as designed, one will obtain the basic abilities of the Korean language in everyday life.

Introduction

This book is designed to help foreigners learn essential Korean in a short period of time and in an effective way. Not only does this book deal with the Korean language but also the Korean culture. This book will be very beneficial for those foreigners who have arrived in Korea recently or for a short period of time. Starting with Hangeul letters, this book directly covers situations which foreigners most frequently cope with in a new environment. Lessons consist of bare essentials that are needed at the beginning stage of life in Korea such as introducing, questioning, giving dates and numbers, ordering food, telephoning, going on a trip, withdrawing money from a bank, shopping, using the drycleaners, and so on.

This book emphasizes the practical use of Korean, not indulging in the detailed explanation of grammar. However, basic grammar is not ignored, but given in a simple and easy way. In each lesson, several grammar points are explained to help organize the learning of the language. However, the explanation is not exhaustive and comprehensive, but related with the dialogs in the given lesson for the purpose of easiness of learning for the beginners without excessive confusion caused by grammar.

In learning foreign languages, practice is the most important factor for learners to digest the new language system. That is why the exercise sections are carefully designed for the practice of each lesson. All questions are introduced based on the prior knowledge acquired from the previous lessons. A few new words related to the given lesson are used for awareness of learners within the range of capability of handling. Hence, using exercises leads to the completion and confirmation of new information from each lesson.

Increasing vocabulary is needed to obtain language abilities. New words are introduced right after dialogs. The derived form of words are given as they are, not to confuse the learners with too many conjugated forms. Word drills are given, when the category of a word needs to be introduced. For example, when you have the word "summer" in a lesson, all words in the category "season" such as fall, winter, and spring are introduced in the Word Drills section. One thing that is worth mentioning is that a lot of pictures are given to help understand the words and text.

Preface

With globalization, the world is getting smaller and smaller. In the era of a rapid exchange of information, technology and culture, mutual understanding among countries is essential for survival in the international community. Communication skills are the key to understanding other countries and to be more competitive in the international market. Due to this trend, the Korean language has now become one of the languages needed by the international community. As the role of Korea expands in the field of international politics, the international economy, and culture, the necessity of the Korean language remarkably grows. In accordance with such requirements, this book was written to facilitate foreigners' learning of the Korean language.

For the publication of this book, many people in the different areas became involved in many ways. Not only experts in the Korean language but also experts in other foreign languages such as English, Chinese, and Japanese took part in publishing this book. Ideas from professionals in the other foreign languages were indispensable in writing this book, because the Korean language textbook is another foreign language to the readers in need. We also had proofreaders from the English-speaking countries, Japanese-speaking countries, and other countries to read this book and obtained invaluable comments from them as a way of incorporating both viewpoints of the language professionals and actual readers.

Revising and proofreading drafts was a great deal of work. Cutting, revising and pasting pictures was also a time-consuming job. We are proud of providing a lot of pictures to help understand the text. We thus would like to acknowledge all the efforts of people who were involved in publishing this book. We hope that this text book will be found in many foreigners' bags everywhere in the world.

Suk-Ja Lee, Ph.D.
Former Director of Institute of Continuing Education
Kyung Hee University
March, 1999

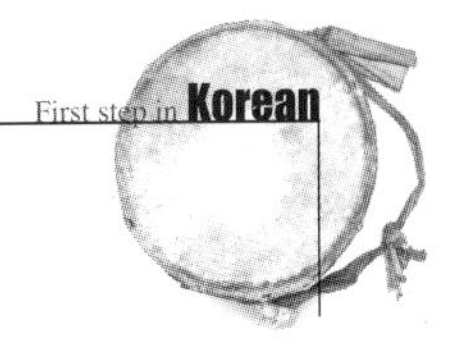

Structures and Expressions

1. The expression '안녕하세요?' is used for greetings when you meet people, meaning 'How are you?'. This expression is also used when you are introduced to people, meaning 'How do you do?'.

2. The subject marker, '~이', is used after a consonant ending in a subject, and the subject marker, '~가', is used after a vowel ending in a subject. For example, 'ㄱ', in '책', and 'ㅁ', in '이름' are consonants, while 'ㅖ' in '시계' and 'ㅜ' in '나무' are vowels, as seen below.

~이 : subject marker	**~가** : subject marker

책이 있습니다. chaegi itseumnida There is a book.	이름이 무엇입니까? ireumi mueosimnikka What's your name?
시계가 있습니다. sigyega itseumnida There is a watch.	나무가 있습니다. namuga itseumnida There is a tree.

3. The topic marker, '~은', is used after a consonant ending in a topic noun, while the topic marker, '~는', is used after a vowel ending in a topic noun. For example, 'ㅁ' in '이름' is a consonant, and 'ㅓ' in '저' and 'ㅣ' in '미' are vowels, as seen below.

~은 : topic marker	**~는** : topic marker

제 이름은 헨리입니다. je ireumeun henriimnida My name is Henry.	나라 이름은 무엇입니까? nara ireumeun mueoshimnikka What is the country' s name?
저는 나이지리아 사람입니다. jeoneun naijiria saramimnida I am a Nigerian.	수미는 한국 사람입니다. sumineun hanguk saramimnida Sumi is a Korean.

4. The 'to be' verb, '~입니다', makes a predication, which attaches to a noun.

~입니다 : *to be* verb

수미입니다.
sumiimnida
I'm Sumi.

케냐 사람입니다.
kenya saramimnida
I'm a Kenyan.

⑤ The question marker, '～까?' makes sentences into a question form, which attaches to the verb stem.

～입니까? : positive question ending
～아닙니까? : negative question ending

어느 나라 사람입니까?
eoneu nara saramimnikka
Which country are you from ?

이름이 무엇입니까?
ireumi mueosimnikka
What's your name?

한국 사람이 아닙니까?
hanguk sarami animnikka
Aren't you a Korean?

⑥ To answer positive Yes-No questions, use '예' for 'yes' and '아니오' for 'no'. For negative questions, '예' is 'no', and '아니오' is 'yes'.

예 : *yes*	**아니오** : *no*

[Positive Yes-No Question]

당신은 미국 사람입니까? Are you from the U.S.A.?
dangshineun miguk saramimnikka

예, 미국 사람입니다. Yes, I'm from the U.S.A.
ye miguk saramimnida

아니오, 미국 사람이 아닙니나. No, I'm not from the U.S.A.
anio miguk sarami animnida

[Negative Yes-No Question]

당신은 미국 사람이 아닙니까? Aren't you from the U.S.A.?
dangsineun miguk sarami animnikka

아니오, 미국 사람입니다. Yes, I'm from the U.S.A.
anio miguk saramimnida

예, 미국 사람이 아닙니다. No, I'm not from the U.S.A.
ye miguk sarami animnida

Exercises

1 Complete the following dialogs using each word in the boxes.

(1) Question : 이름이 무엇이에요?
What is your name?
Answer : 제 이름은 헨리입니다.
My name is Henry.

이수미 isumi
존슨 jonseun
영주 yeongju
야마다 yamada

(2) Question : 당신은 어느 나라 사람입니까?
Which country are you from?
Answer : 저는 나이지리아 사람입니다.
I'm from Nigeria.

미얀마 miyanma
중국 jungguk
한국 hanguk
러시아 reosia

2 Complete the following sentences using appropriate markers provided in the box.

은,	는,	이,	가,	을,	를
eun	neun	i	ga	eul	reul

(1) 제 이름( ) 헨리입니다.
My name is Henry.

(2) 책( ) 있습니다.
There is a book.

(3) 이름( ) 무엇입니까?
What's your name?

(4) 저( ) 나이지리아 사람입니다.
I'm from Nigeria.

(5) 당신( ) 어느 나라 사람입니까?
Which country are you from?

3 Provide an appropriate answer for the following questions.

Example
Q : 당신은 미국 사람입니까? — Are you an American?
A : 예, 저는 미국 사람입니다. — Yes, I'm an American.
아니오, 저는 미국 사람이 아닙니다. — No, I'm not an American.

(1) 당신은 나이지리아 사람입니까? (예) ______________________.
Are you from Nigeria?

(2) 당신은 한국 사람입니까? (아니오) ________.
Are you from Korea?

(3) 당신은 미얀마 사람입니까? (예) ________.
Are you from Myanmar?

(4) 당신은 중국 사람입니까? (예 / 아니오) ________.
Are you from China?

(5) 당신은 일본 사람입니까? (예 / 아니오) ________.
Are you from Japan?

Reading Practice

(1) 당신의 이름은 무엇입니까?
What's your name?

(2) 제 이름은 이수미입니다.
My name is Lee Sumi.

(3) 만나서 반갑습니다. 안녕히 계세요.
Nice meeting you. Good-bye.

(4) 당신은 어느 나라 사람입니까?
Which country are you from?

(5) 저는 한국 사람입니다.
I am a Korean.

노란색 ○	yellow	검은색 ●	black
빨간색 ●	red	흰 색 ○	white
파란색 ●	blue	분홍색 ●	pink
보라색 ●	purple	초록색 ●	green
회 색 ●	gray	연두색 ●	yellowish green
주황색 ●	orange	하늘색 ○	sky blue

제 2 과
Lesson 2

아버지의 직업은 무엇입니까?
What's Your Father's Occupation?

Key Sentences

1. 아버지의 직업은 무엇입니까? — What's your father's occupation?
   abeojiui jigeobeun mueosimnikka
2. 당신은 지금 무엇을 합니까? — Currently, what do you do?
   dangsineun jigeum mueoseul hamnikka

Dialogs

Dialog 1

수미: 당신의 가족을 소개해 주세요.
dangsinui gajogeul sogaehae juseyo
Please introduce your family to me.

헨리: 아버지, 어머니, 형, 동생이 있습니다.
abeoji eomeoni hyeong dongsaeng-i itseumnida
I have a father, mother, elder brother, and younger brother.

수미: 아버지의 직업은 무엇입니까?
abeojiui jigeobeun mueosimnikka
What's your father's occupation?

헨리: 회사원입니다. He is an office worker.
hoesawonimnida

Dialog 2

수미: 당신은 지금 무엇을 합니까?
dangsineun jigeum mueoseul hamnikka
Currently, what do you do?

헨리: 저는 태평양 대학교에서 한국어를 배웁니다.
jeoneun taepyeongyang daehakgyoeseo hangugeoreul baeumnida
I am studying Korean at Taepyeongyang University.

수미: 한국어는 재미있습니까?
hangugeoneun jaemiitseumnikka
Is Korean interesting?

헨리: 네, 어렵지만 재미있습니다.
ne eoryeopjiman jaemiitseumnida
Yes, it's difficult, but interesting.

수미: 한국인 친구가 있습니까?
hangugin chin-guga itseumnikka
Do you have any Korean friends?

헨리: 네, 많습니다.
ne mansseumnida.
Yes, I have many.

Vocabulary and Phrases

- 당신의 your
- 소개하다 to introduce
- 아버지 father
- 형 elder brother
- 직업 job, occupation
- 지금 now
- 대학교 university
- 배우다 to learn
- 한국인 Korean
- 많습니다 a lot of/many/much
- 가족 family
- 주다/주세요 to give
- 어머니 mother
- 남동생 younger brother
- 회사원 office worker
- 무엇을 합니까? What are you doing?
- 한국어 Korean language
- 재미있다 to be interesting
- 친구 friend
- 적습니다 a little/a few

Word Drills

할아버지
harabeoji
grandfather

할머니
halmeoni
grandmother

아버지
abeoji
father

어머니
eomeoni
mother

오빠 elder brother to a female
oppa
형 elder brother to a male
hyeong

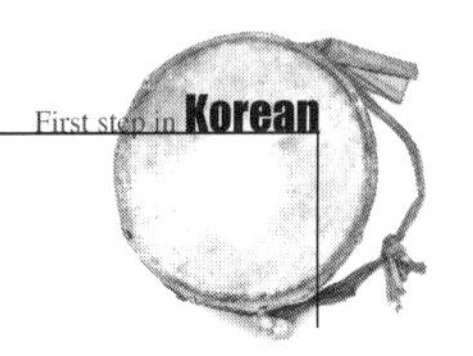

언니 elder sister to a female
eonni
누나 elder sister to a male
nuna

남동생 younger brother
namdongsaeng

여동생 younger sister
yeodongsaeng

의사 doctor
uisa

간호사 nurse
ganhosa

경찰관 police officer
gyeongchalgwan

소방관 fire fighter
sobanggwan

아나운서 announcer
anaunseo

가수 singer
gasu

Structures and Expressions

① A possessive marker '~의' is attached to a noun, indicating that the noun is a possessor.

~의 : possessive marker

당신의 가족
dangsinui gajok
your family

나의 직업
naui jigeop
my job

수미의 언니
sumiui eonni
Sumi's sister

자연의 아름다움
jayeonui areumdaum
beauty of nature

② An object marker '~을' is used after a noun when the noun ends with a consonant, while '~를' is used when the noun ends with a vowel.

가족을 : family	**아버지를** : father

가족을 소개해 주세요.
gajogeul sogaehae juseyo
Please introduce your family.

아버지를 소개해 주세요.
abeojireul sogaehae juseyo
Please introduce your father.

③ '무엇' is one of the question words, meaning 'what'. Case markers follow the question word, and '~까?' is attached in the sentence-final position to make a question.

무엇을 합니까? : What do you do?

지금 무엇을 합니까?
jigeum mueoseul hamnikka
Currently, what do you do?

당신은 무엇을 합니까?
dangsineun mueoseul hamnikka
What do you do?

친구는 무엇을 합니까?
chin-guneun mueoseul hamnikka
What does your friend do?

④ The polite formal style is expressed with the following sentence endings in statements and questions respectively. '~ㅂ니다/ㅂ니까?' is used when verb stems end in a vowel, and '~습니다/습니까?' is used when verb stems end in a consonant.

~ㅂ니다/습니다 : to be
~ㅂ니까?/습니까? : question form

이다. ida	입니다. imnida	to be	있다. itda	있습니다. itseumnida	to exist
	입니까? imnikka			있습니까? itseumnikka	

⑤ '저' is the honorific word of a first person pronoun '나 (I)'. In Korean, there are the honorific counterparts of the person pronouns as below.

	singular	honorific	plural	honorific
1st person	나 na	저 jeo	우리들 urideul	저희들 jeohuideul
2nd person	너 neo	당신 dangsin	너희들 neohuideul	당신들 dangsindeul
3rd person	그 geu	그분 geubun	그들 geudeul	그분들 geubundeul

⑥ '~지만' is attached to the first verb or adjective in conjoined verbs or adjective phrases, meaning 'but'.

~지만 : although, but

어렵지만 재미있습니다. It is difficult, but interesting.
eoryeopjiman jaemiitseumnida

힘들지만 재미있습니다. It is hard, but interesting.
himdeuljiman jaemiitseumnida

Exercises

1 Complete the following dialogs using each word in the boxes. (1)~(4)

(1) 아버지의 직업은 무엇입니까? What is your father's occupation?

Example
어머니 eomeoni 할아버지 harabeoji 할머니 halmeoni 형 hyeong 동생 dongsaeng

(2) 아버지의 직업은 의사입니다. My father is a doctor.

Example
선생님 seonsaengnim 운전기사 unjeongisa 회사원 hoesawon
경찰관 gyeongchalgwan 소방관 sobanggwan

(3) 한국어는 재미있습니까? Is the Korean language interesting?

Example
중국어 junggugeo 영어 yeong-eo 일본어 ilboneo 미얀마 어 miyanmaeo 러시아 어 reosiaeo

(4) 친구가/이 많습니다. I have many friends.

Example
나라 nara 형 hyeong 가족 gajok 회사 hoesa 동생 dongsaeng

2 Change the following expressions into the polite formal style as shown in the example.

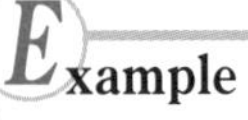
xample
회사원이다. → 회사원입니다. I am an office worker.

한국어를 배우다. → ______________________

동생이 있다. → ______________________

재미있다. → ______________________

많다. → ______________________

Reading Practice

(1) 형의 직업은 무엇이에요?
What's your elder brother's occupation?

(2) 헨리, 지금 무엇을 해요? Henry, what do you do now?

(3) 저는 태평양 대학교에서 한국어를 배워요.
I'm studying the Korean language at Taepyeongyang University.

(4) 저는 한국인 친구가 많습니다. I have many Korean friends.

(5) 한국어는 재미있습니다. The Korean language is interesting.

제 3 과

어디 있어요? Where Is It?

Key Sentences

1. 화장실이 어디 있어요? Where's the restroom?
   hwajangsiri eodi isseoyo
2. 약국 오른쪽에 있어요. It's on the right side of the drugstore.
   yakguk oreunjjoge isseoyo

Dialogs

Dialog 1

헨리: 실례합니다. 화장실이 어디 있어요?
sillyehamnida hwajangsiri eodi isseoyo
Excuse me. Where's the restroom?

남자: 저기 약국이 보여요?
jeogi yakgugi boyeoyo
Can you see the drugstore over there?

헨리: 네, 보여요.
ne, boyeoyo
Yes, I can.

남자: 약국 오른쪽에 있어요.
yakguk oreunjjoge isseoyo
It's on the right side of the drugstore.

헨리: 고맙습니다.
gomapseumnida
Thank you.

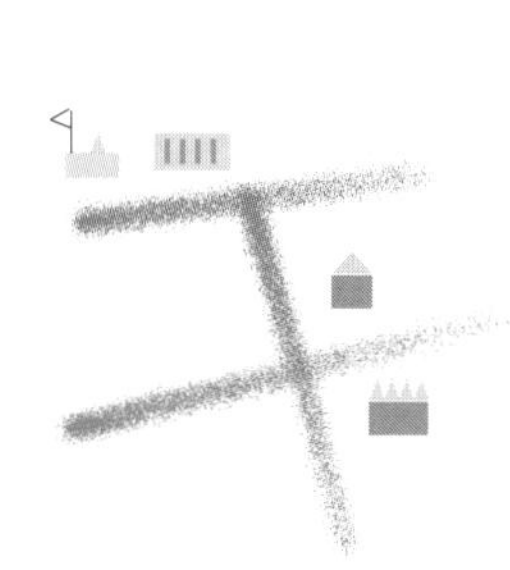

Dialog 2

헨리: 실례합니다. 경찰서가 어디 있어요?
sillyehamnida gyeongchalseoga eodi isseoyo
Excuse me. Where's the police station?

지갑을 잃어버렸어요.
jigabeul ireobeoryeosseoyo
I lost my wallet.

남자: 저 쪽으로 한 블록 가세요.
jeo jjogeuro han beulleok gaseyo
Just go one block that way.

대한 슈퍼 옆에 있어요.
daehan syupeo yeope isseoyo
It's next to the Daehan supermarket.

헨리: 감사합니다.
gamsahamnida
Thank you.

Vocabulary and Phrases

• 실례합니다	excuse me	• 약국	drugstore	• 이쪽	this way
• 감사합니다	thank you	• 보다	to see	• 저쪽	that way
• 고맙습니다	thank you	• 오른쪽에	on the right	• 옆에	next to
• 화장실	restroom	• 왼쪽에	on the left	• 한	one
• 어디	where	• 경찰서	police station	• 블록	block
• 있다	there is	• 지갑	wallet	• 있어요?	Is there...?
• 가다/가세요	to go	• 잃어버리다	to lose	• 저기	there
• 잃어버렸어요	lost	• 대한슈퍼	Daehan supermarket		

Word Drills

방향에 관한 단어 (Direction Words)

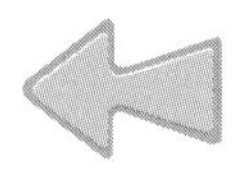

왼쪽 the left side
oenjjok

오른쪽 the right side
oreunjjok

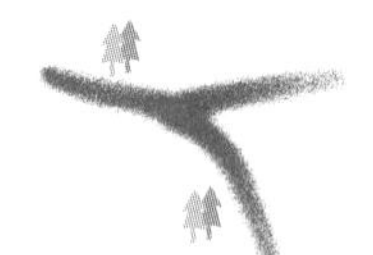

저쪽 that way
jeojjok

이쪽 this way
ijjok

위치에 관한 단어 (Location Words)

앞 front
ap

뒤 behind
dwi

옆 next to
yeop

위 on
wi

아래 under
arae

안 in
an

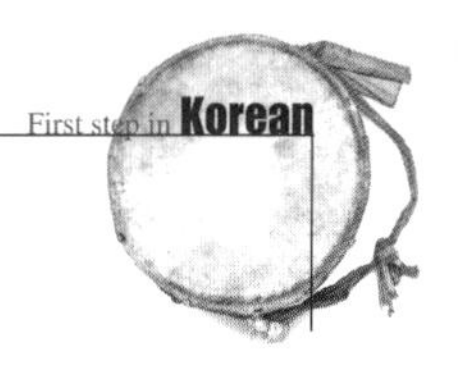

Structures and Expressions

① To form a question, add '∼요?' with a rising intonation. '∼요?' makes the polite informal style, while '∼까?' makes the polite formal style.

∼ 있다/있어요? : (Where) is ∼.	**보이다/보여요?** : Can you see ∼ ?

화장실이 어디 있어요?
hwajangsiri eodi isseoyo
Where is the restroom?

약국이 보여요?
yakgugi boyeoyo
Can you see the drugstore?

② The question word '어디' is used to ask about a place.

어디 있어요? : Where is it ?

어디 있어요?
eodi isseoyo
Where is it?

어디 가세요?
eodi gaseyo
Where are you going?

③ To make a statement, add '∼요' with a falling intonation. '∼요' makes the polite informal style, while '∼ㅂ니다/습니다' makes the polite formal style.

∼ 있어요. : It is ∼.

오른쪽에 있어요.
oreunjjoge isseoyo
It is on the right.

슈퍼 앞에 있어요.
syupeo ape isseoyo
It is in front of the supermarket.

④ When you want to express 'Thank you', use '고맙습니다' or '감사합니다'. When you want to get someone's attention, use '실례합니다'. Use '괜찮습니다' to express 'It's OK' and use '좋습니다' for 'It is good'.

고맙습니다. : Thank you.	**감사합니다.** : Thank you.
실례합니다. : Excuse me.	**괜찮습니다.** : It is OK.
좋습니다. : It is good.	

⑤ '∼어' in '잃어' is a sequential marker used to connect two verbs. '∼었' in '버렸어요' is a past tense marker.

∼ 잃어버리다 / 잃어버렸어요. : to lose / lost

잃다+버리다 → 잃어버리다 lose
ilta+beorida ireobeorida

잃어버리+었+어요 → 잃어버렸어요 lost
ireobeori+eot+eoyo ireobeoryeosseoyo

죽다+버리다 → 죽어버리다 die
jukda+beorida jugeobeorida

죽어버리+었+어요 → 죽어버렸어요 died
jugeobeori+eot+eoyo jugeobeoryeosseoyo

6 '~시' is a honorific marker used after verb stems.

가다 / 가세요 : to go / please go

가(다)+시+어요 → 가세요 Please go.
gaseyo

오(다)+시+어요 → 오세요 Please come.
oseyo

Exercises

1 Complete the following dialogs using each word in the box.

Example

- 강의실 classroom
- 백화점 department store
- 공중전화 public phone
- 편의점 convenience store
- 동사무소 public town office
- 은행 bank
- 모텔 motel
- 사무실 office
- 우체국 post office
- 버스정류장 bus station
- 지하철 subway
- 공장 factory
- 병원 hospital
- 공원 park

(1) ________이/가 어디 있어요? ________이/가 어디 있어요?
(2) ________이/가 어디 있어요? ________이/가 어디 있어요?
(3) ________이/가 어디 있어요? ________이/가 어디 있어요?
(4) ________이/가 어디 있어요? ________이/가 어디 있어요?

Exercises

2 Complete the following sentences with direction words.

(1) ________에 있어요. (2) ________에 있습니다.

(3) ________에 있어요. (4) ________에 있습니다.

(5) ________에 있어요. (6) ________에 있습니다.

3 Complete the following sentences with location words.

(1) ________에 있어요. (2) ________에 있습니다.

(3) ________에 있어요. (4) ________에 있습니다.

(5) ________에 있어요. (6) ________에 있습니다.

4 Complete the following dialogs with appropriate words.

가: 공원이 ____________?
나: ____________에 있어요.

가: ____________이 어디 있어요?
나: 왼쪽에 ____________.

Reading Practice

(1) 동사무소가 어디 있어요? Where is the public town office?

(2) 저쪽으로 가세요. Please go that way.

(3) 슈퍼 오른쪽에 있어요. It is on the right side of the supermarket.

(4) 가방을 잃어버렸어요. I lost my bag.

(5) 경찰서 앞에 있어요. It's in front of the police station.

NATIONAL HOLIDAYS (공휴일) [gonghyu-il]

- **설날** [seolnal] (January 1 by the lunar calendar: Lunar New Year's Day)
  The first day of the first lunar month is the biggest Korean holiday, which is called 'Seol' (설) in Korean. All the family are dressed in traditional clothes 'Hanbok' (한복) and observe ancestral rites.

- **3·1절** [samiljeol] (March 1: Independence Movement Day)
  This day commemorates the Declaration of Independence that was proclaimed on March 1, 1919, while the nation was under Japanese colonization. A reading of the declaration takes place during a special ceremony in Tapgol Park.

- **식목일** [sikmogil] (April 5: Arbor Day)
  Trees are planted across the country as part of the nation's vast reforestation program.

- **어린이날** [eorininal] (May 5: Children's Day)
  This day is celebrated with various programs for children. Parks, zoos, and amusement parks are crowded with excited and colorfully dressed children.

- **석가탄신일** [seokgatansinil] (April 8 by the lunar calendar: Buddha's Birthday)
  Elaborate and solemn rituals are held at many Buddhist temples across the country and lanterns are displayed in the streets and in temple courtyards. In the evening these lanterns are carried in parades.

- **광복절** [gwangbokjeol] (August 15: Liberation Day)
  This day commemorates the Japanese acceptance of the Allied terms of surrender and the resulting liberation of Korea in 1945.

- **추석** [chuseok] (August 15 by the lunar calendar: the Korean Thanksgiving Day)
  This day is the most important traditional holiday of the year. It is celebrated on the 15th day of the eighth lunar month to celebrate the harvest and to give thanks for the bounty of the earth. People visit their family tombs to present offerings to their ancestors with the year's new crops and fruits.

- **크리스마스** [keurismas] (December 25: Christmas)
  Christmas is observed as a national holiday in Korea, as in most other countries.

제 4 과
Lesson 4

이것은 한국어로 무엇입니까?
What Is This in Korean?

Key Sentences

1. 이것은 무엇입니까? — What is this?
   igeoseun mueosimnikka
2. 이것은 한국어로 무엇입니까? — What is this in Korean?
   igeoseun hangugeoro mueosimnikka

Dialogs

Dialog 1

헨리: 이것은 무엇입니까?
igeoseun mueosimnikka
What are these?

수미: 그것은 운동화입니다.
geugeoseun undonghwaimnida
Those are sneakers.

헨리: 그러면, 저것은 무엇이에요?
geureomyeon jeogeoseun mueosieyo
Then, what's that?

수미: 가방입니다. It's a bag.
gabang-imnida

헨리: 가방이 예쁘군요. The bag is pretty.
gabang-i yeppeugunyo

Dialog 2

헨리: 이것은 한국어로 무엇입니까?
igeoseun hangugeoro mueosimnikka
What is this in Korean?

수미: 목걸이입니다. It is 목걸이.
mokgeoriimnida

헨리: 이것은 한국어로 바지입니까?
igeoseun hangugeoro bajiimnikka
Is this 바지 in Korean?

수미: 아니오, 그것은 바지가 아닙니다.
anio geugeoseun bajiga animnida
No, it's not 바지.

치마입니다.
chimaimnida
It's 치마.

Vocabulary and Phrases

• 이것	this	• 운동화	sneakers	• 가방	bag
• 저것	that	• 그러면	then	• 아니오	no
• 무엇	what	• 목걸이	necklace	• 아닙니다	not
• 이다/입니다	to be	• 한국어로	in Korean	• 치마	skirt
• 이에요?	Is it...?	• 한국어	Korean language	• 바지	pants
• 무엇입니까?	What is...?	• 예쁘다	to be pretty		

Word Drills

Personal Belongings

시계
sigye
watch

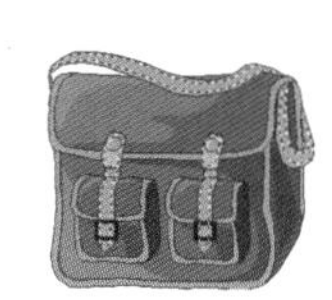

가방
gabang
bag

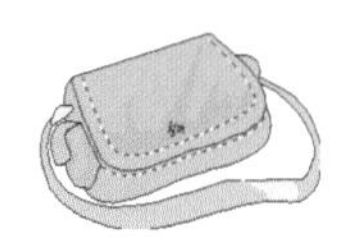

핸드백
haendbaek
purse

지갑
jigap
purse, wallet

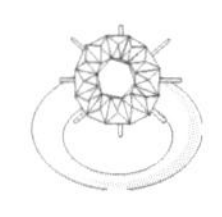

반지
banji
ring

목걸이
mokgeori
necklace

팔찌
paljji
bracelet

Kinds of Shoes

운동화
undonghwa
sneakers

구두
gudu
shoes

부츠
bucheu
boots

슬리퍼
seulripeo
slippers

샌들
saendeul
sandals

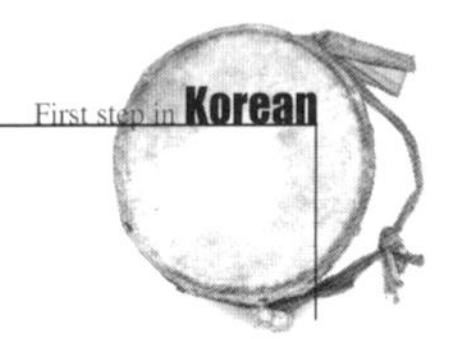

Kinds of clothes

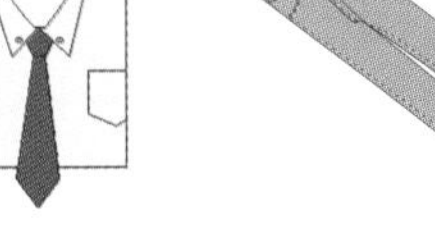

셔츠	바지	원피스	투피스	양복	잠옷
syeocheu	baji	wonpis	tupis	yangbok	jamot
shirt	pants	dress	two-piece suit	suit	pajamas

블라우스	재킷	치마	코트	운동복
beulraus	jaekit	chima	kot	undongbok
blouse	jacket	skirt	coat	sports wear

Korean Traditional Clothes

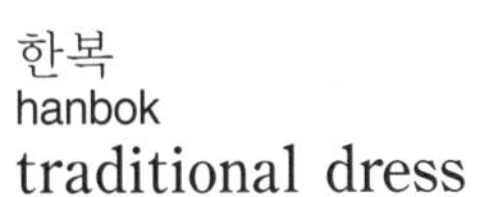
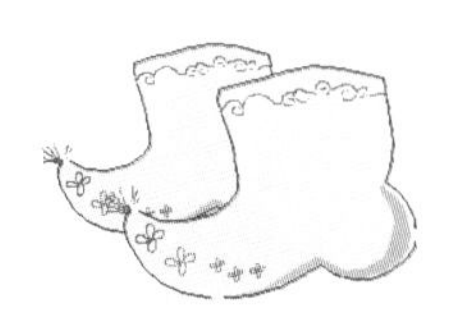
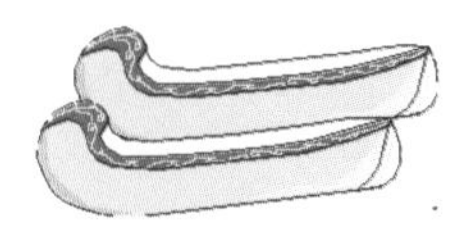
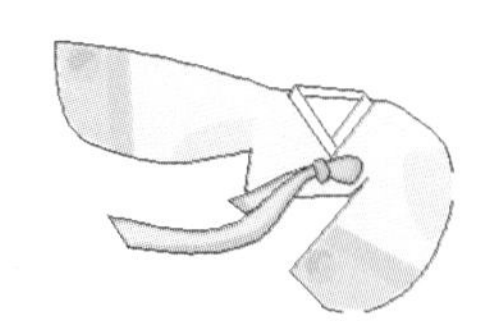

한복	버선	고무신	고름
hanbok	beoseon	gomusin	goreum
traditional dress	socks	rubber shoes	tie

Structures and Expressions

① There are three distinctive ways of Korean demonstratives: (i) '이것' is used for a thing which is close to the speaker, (ii) '그것' is used for a thing which is close to the listener, and (iii) '저것' is used for a thing which is far away from both the speaker and listener.

이것 : this	**그것** : it	**저것** : that

이것은 무엇입니까?
igeoseun mueosimnikka
What is this?

저것은 무엇입니까?
jeogeoseun mueosimnikka
What is that?

그것은 무엇입니까? What is it?
geugeoseun mueosimnikka

② The question ending '~이에요?' is used for the polite informal style, while '~입니까?' is used for the polite formal style in question ending.

무엇입니까? : What is it?	**무엇이에요?** : What is it?

이것은 무엇입니까?
igeoseun mueosimnikka
What is this?

이것은 무엇이에요?
igeoseun mueosieyo
What is this?

③ When you form a question from a statement, attach '~까?' in the sentence-final position for the polite formal style, and attach '~요' in the same position for the polite informal style. Note that the polite sentence ending '~요' is the same for both a statement and a question, but is different only in tone: '~요' in a statement has a falling intonation, while '~요' in a question has a rising intonation.

> **이것은 바지입니까?** : Are these pants?
> **이것은 바지예요?** : Are these pants?

이것은 바지입니다. → 이것은 바지입니까?
igeoseun bajiimnida → igeoseun bajiimnikka
These are pants. → Are these pants?

이것은 바지예요. → 이것은 바지예요?
igeoseun bajiiyeo → igeoseun bajiyeyo
These are pants. → Are these pants?

④ The sentence ending '~군' indicates the speaker's new awareness of a fact or an event. With '~요' attached to '~군', the sentence ending is made polite.

> **예쁘군. → 예쁘군요.** : How pretty it is!

예쁘다.	예쁘군.	예쁘군요.
yeppeuda	yeppeugun	yeppeugunyo
How pretty it is!		
아름답다.	아름답군.	아름답군요.
areumdapda	areumdapgun	areumdapgunyo
How beautiful it is!		

⑤ When you want to express 'No', use '아니오'. To change a positive statement into a negative form, use '~이/~가 아닙니다'.

> **아니오, 이것은 바지가 아닙니다.** : No, these are not pants.

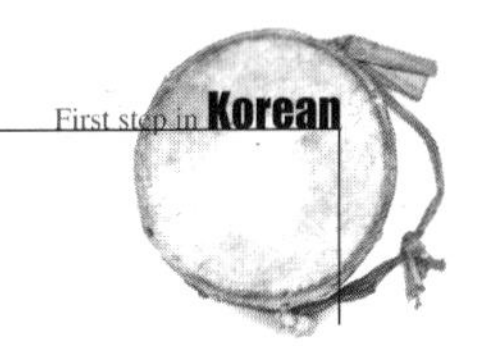

아니오, 이것은 치마가 아닙니다. No, this is not a skirt.
anio igeoseun chimaga animnida

아니오, 이것은 목걸이가 아닙니다. No, this is not a necklace.
anio igeoseun mokgeoriga animnida

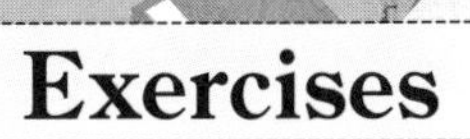

Exercises

1 Provide answers for the questions in the box using words in parenthesis.

Question
Q1 : 이것은 무엇입니까? What is this?
Q2 : 저것은 무엇입니까? What is that?

(1) 그것은 ____________ .(한복 traditional Korean clothes)
(2) 저것은 ____________ .(색동저고리 colorful traditional shirt)
(3) 그것은 ____________ .(치마 skirt)
(4) 저것은 ____________ .(버선 traditional socks)

2 Complete the following sentences as shown in the example.

Example
이것은 시계입니다. This is a watch.

(1) ________ 목걸이 ____________.
(2) ________ 반지 ____________.
(3) ________ 바지 ____________.
(4) ________ 치마 ____________.
(5) ________ 운동화 ____________.
(6) ________ 가방 ____________.

3 Complete the sentences below following the example in the box.

Example
pen은 한국어로 무엇입니까? What is a pen in Korean?

(1) skirt는 한국어로 ____________?
(2) pants는 한국어로 ____________?
(3) necklace는 한국어로 ________?
(4) bag은 한국어로 ____________?

4 Change the following sentences into question forms as shown in the example.

Exemple

이것은 한국어로 운동화입니다. This is 운동화 in Korean.
→ 이것은 한국어로 운동화입니까? Is this 운동화 in Korean?

(1) 이것은 한국어로 컴퓨터입니다. This is 컴퓨터 in Korean.
→ ______________________________

(2) 이것은 한국어로 프린터입니다. This is 프린터 in Korean.
→ ______________________________

(3) 이것은 한국어로 모니터입니다. This is 모니터 in Korean.
→ ______________________________

(4) 이것은 한국어로 키보드입니다. This is 키보드 in Korean.
→ ______________________________

5 Change the following sentences into negative forms.

(1) 이것은 치마입니다. This is a skirt.
→ ______________________________

(2) 이것은 바지입니다. These are pants.
→ ______________________________

(3) 이것은 재킷입니다. This is a jacket.
→ ______________________________

(4) 이것은 양복입니다. This is a suit.
→ ______________________________

Reading Practice

(1) 이것은 운동화입니다. These are sneakers.

(2) 저것은 컵이 아닙니다. That is not a cup.

(3) 이것은 한국어로 무엇입니까? What is this in Korean?

(4) 저것은 접시, 포크, 나이프입니다. Those are a dish, a fork, and a knife.

(5) 이 접시는 참 예쁘군요. This dish is very pretty.

제 5 과

Lesson 5

어느 계절을 좋아해요?

Which Season Do You Like?

Key Sentences

1. 어느 계절을 좋아해요? — Which season do you like?
   eoneu gyejeoreul joahaeyo
2. 오늘은 날씨가 흐리군요. — It is cloudy today.
   oneureun nalssiga heurigunyo

Dialogs

Dialog 1

수미: 헨리 씨는 어느 계절을 좋아해요?
henri ssineun eoneu gyejeoreul joahaeyo
Henry, which season do you like?

헨리: 가을을 좋아해요.
gaeureul joahaeyo
I like fall.

가을은 시원해요.
gaeureun siwonhaeyo
Fall is cool.

수미: 어느 계절을 싫어해요?
eoneu gyejeoreul sireohaeyo
Which season do you dislike?

헨리: 겨울을 싫어해요.
gyeoureul sireohaeyo
I dislike winter.

겨울은 추워요.
gyeoureun chuwoyo
Winter is cold.

Dialog 2

수미: 오늘은 날씨가 흐리군요.
oneureun nalssiga heurigeunyo
It is cloudy today.

헨리: 비가 올 것 같아요.
biga ol geot gatayo
It looks like rain.

수미: 우산 가져왔어요?
usan gajyeowasseoyo
Did you bring an umbrella?

헨리: 네, 가져왔어요.
ne gajyeowasseoyo
Yes, I did.

일기예보를 보았어요.
ilgi yeboreul boasseoyo
I read the weather forecast.

Vocabulary and Phrases

- 어느 which
- 좋아해요 like
- 춥다 cold
- 오늘 today
- 비 rain
- 가을 fall, autumn
- 시원하다 to be cool, refreshing
- 흐리다 to be cloudy/overcast
- 일기 예보 a weather forecast
- 계절 season
- 덥다 to be hot
- 날씨 weather
- 겨울 winter
- 우산 umbrella
- 싫어해요 dislike
- ~인 것 같아요 It seems that
- 보다/보았어요 to see/saw
- 가져오다/가져왔어요 to bring/brought

Word Drills

Four seasons

봄 spring
bom

여름 summer
yeoreum

가을 fall
gaeul

겨울 winter
gyeoul

Weather

해
hae
sun

맑은
malgeun
clear

구름
gureum
cloud

흐린
heurin
cloudy

비
bi
rain

눈
nun
snow

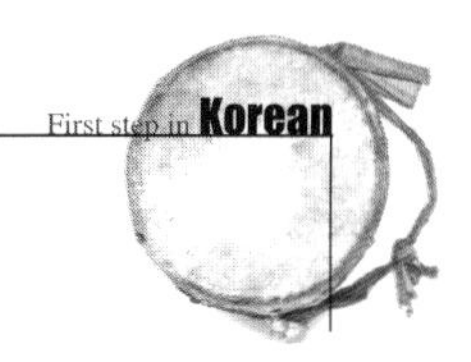

Structures and Expressions

① The question word '어느' is used to ask about a choice.

> **어느** : which

어느 계절을 좋아해요?
eoneu gyejeoreul joahaeyo
Which season do you like?

어느 모자를 좋아해요?
eoneu mojareul joahaeyo
Which hat do you like?

② The past tense markers, '~았/었' are attached after verb stems. '~았' is attached after a verb whose stem vowel is either '아' or '오', while '~었' is used after all other stem vowels. '~였' is analyzed as '이+었', where '이' is inserted for pronunciation purpose.

> **~았 / 었 / 였** : 과거시제 (past tense)

보았어요 saw
boasseoyo

알았어요 knew
arasseoyo

먹었어요 ate
meogeosseoyo

배웠어요 learned
baewosseoyo

하였어요 did
hayeosseoyo

note '웠' in '배웠어요' is analyzed as '우(verb stem vowel)+었(past tense marker)'.

③ Construction of '~것 같다' indicates an opinion of the speaker, preceded by a verbal modifier.

> **~것 같다 / ~것 같아요** : It seems that....

비가 올 것 같아요.
biga ol geot gatayo
It seems that it will rain.

눈이 올 것 같아요.
nuni ol geot gatayo
It seems that it will snow.

존이 한 것 같아요.
joni han geot gatayo
It appears that John did it.

④ '~ㄹ/~ㄴ', followed by a verb stem makes the verb into a verbal modifier. '~ㄹ' indicates a future tense, and '~ㄴ' indicates a past tense.

올 것 같아요 : It seems that it will ....
온 것 같아요 : It seems that it did ....

비가 올 것 같아요.
biga ol geot gatayo
It seems that it will rain.

비가 온 것 같아요.
biga on geot gatayo
It seems that it has rained.

⑤ Expressions related with seasons are as follows.

봄은 따뜻합니다.
bomeun ttatteuthamnida
Spring is warm.

여름은 덥습니다.
yeoreumeun deopseumnida
Summer is hot.

가을은 시원합니다.
gaeureun siwonhamnida
Fall is cool.

겨울은 춥습니다.
gyeoureun chupsseumnida
Winter is cold.

⑥ Expressions related with weather are as follows.

비가 옵니다.
biga omnida
It is raining.

눈이 옵니다.
nuni omnida
It is snowing.

바람이 붑니다.
barami bumnida
It is windy.

천둥이 칩니다.
cheondung-i chimnida
It is thundering.

⑦ Attach '~씨', when you call a person's name. This is the polite way of calling an adult's name. But you shouldn't attach this suffix to children's names.

수미 씨
sumi ssi
Sumi

헨리 씨
henri ssi
Henry

Exercises

1 Provide answers for the following questions.

uestions

Q 1 : 당신은 어느 계절을 좋아해요? Which season do you like?
Q 2 : 당신은 어느 계절을 싫어해요? Which season do you dislike?

저는 봄 / 여름 / 가을 / 겨울 을 좋아해요.
I like ... (   ).

저는 봄 / 여름 / 가을 / 겨울 을 싫어해요.
I dislike ... (   ).

2 Complete the following sentences as shown in the example.

Example

Q : 오늘 날씨가 어때요?(춥다) How's the weather today?
A : 오늘 날씨는 추워요. It is cold.

(1) 흐리다 cloudy
(2) 덥다 hot
(3) 비가 오다 raining
(4) 맑다 clear
(5) 눈이 오다 snowing

3 Complete the sentences below following the example in the box.

Example

Q : 우산을 가져왔어요? (우산) Did you bring your umbrella?

(1) 책 book
(2) 가방 bag
(3) 펜 pen
(4) 시계 watch
(5) 휴지 tissues

4 Change the following sentences into a past tense form.

(1) 일기 예보를 보다 to read the weather forecast

(2) 밥을 먹다 to eat rice

(3) 학교에 가다 to go to school

(4) 가을을 좋아하다 to like fall

(5) 친구를 만나다 to meet friends

Reading Practice

(1) 어느 계절을 좋아해요?
Which season do you like?

(2) 오늘은 날씨가 흐리군요.
It's cloudy today.

(3) 여름은 너무 더워요.
Summer is very hot.

(4) 우산을 가져왔어요.
I've brought an umbrella.

(5) 저는 겨울을 싫어해요.
I dislike winter.

제 6 과
Lesson 6

생일이 언제예요?
When Is Your Birthday?

Key Sentences

1. 오늘은 금요일이에요. — Today is Friday.
   oneureun geumyoirieyo
2. 제 생일은 5월 23일이에요. — My birthday is on May 23rd.
   je saeng-ireun owol isipsamirieyo

Dialogs

Dialog 1

헨리: 어제는 무엇을 했어요?
eojeneun mueoseul haesseoyo
What did you do yesterday?

수미: 어제는 도서관에서 공부를 했어요.
eojeneun doseogwaneseo gongbureul haesseoyo
I studied at the library yesterday.

헨리: 오늘은 무슨 요일이에요?
oneureun museun yoirieyo
What day is it today?

수미: 오늘은 금요일이에요.
oneureun geumyoirieyo
Today is Friday.

헨리: 내일은 학교에 갈 거예요?
naeireun hakgyoe gal geoyeyo
Are you going to go to school tomorrow?

수미: 아니오, 내일은 집에 있을 거예요.
anio naeireun jibe isseul geoyeyo
No, I'm going to stay at home.

5월

일 (SUN)	월 (MON)	화 (TUE)	수 (WED)	목 (THU)	금 (FRI)	토 (SAT)
	1	2	3	4	5	6
7	8	9	10	11	12	13
14	15	16	17	18	19	20
21	22	23	24	25	26	27
28	29	30	31			

Dialog 2

헨리: 수미 씨, 생일이 언제예요?
sumi ssi saeng-iri eonjeyeyo
Sumi, when is your birthday?

수미: 제 생일은 5월 23일이에요.
je saeng-ireun owol isipsamirieyo
My birthday is on May 23rd.

헨리: 모레군요. 우리 생일 파티해요.
moregunnyo uri saeng-il patihaeyo
It's the day after tomorrow. Let's have a birthday party!

수미: 모레 저녁 7시에 우리 집에 오세요.
more jeonyeok ilgopsie uri jibe oseyo
Come to my house the day after tomorrow at 7 P.M.

Vocabulary and Phrases

- 어제 yesterday
- 무슨, 무엇 what
- 언제 when
- 일, 요일 day
- 내일 tomorrow
- 갈 거예요? will (you) go?
- 집 home, house
- 오다/오세요 to come
- 모레 the day after tomorrow
- 우리~해요 let's
- 생일파티 birthday party
- 생일 birthday
- 7시 7 o'clock
- 도서관 library
- ~에서 in, at
- 오늘 today
- 금요일 Friday
- 아니오 no
- ~에 at
- 23일 23rd
- 저녁 evening
- 우리 we, our
- 학교 school
- 공부 study
- 5월 May

Word Drills

Days

일요일 iryoil	월요일 woryoil	화요일 hwayoil	수요일 suyoil	목요일 mogyoil	금요일 geumyoil	토요일 toyoil
Sunday	Monday	Tuesday	Wednesday	Thursday	Friday	Saturday

그저께(geujeokke)	the day before yesterday
어제(eoje)	yesterday
오늘(oneul)	today
내일(naeil)	tomorrow
모레(more)	the day after tomorrow

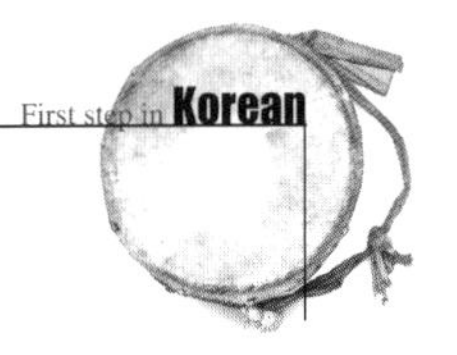

Months

1월	January	일월(irwol)	7월	July	칠월(chirwol)
2월	February	이월(iwol)	8월	August	팔월(parwol)
3월	March	삼월(samwol)	9월	September	구월(guwol)
4월	April	사월(sawol)	10월	October	시월(siwol)
5월	May	오월(owol)	11월	November	십일월(sibirwol)
6월	June	유월(yuwol)	12월	December	십이월(sibiwol)

Structures and Expressions

1. '무슨' is the modifying form of '무엇' preceded by a noun, meaning 'what' in English.

무슨 요일이에요? : What day is it (today)?

이것은 무엇입니까?
igeoseun mueosimnikka
What is this?

오늘은 무슨 요일이에요?
oneureun museun yoirieyo
What day is it today?

2. The polite informal sentence ending '~이에요' is used when a word ends with a consonant, while '~예요' is used when a word ends with a vowel. Both endings are used for either a statement or a question. '~예요' is a contracted form of '~이에요' in pronunciation.

언제예요? : When is it? **23일이에요.** : It is the 23rd.

생일이 언제예요?
saeng-iri eonjeyeyo
When is your birthday?

제 생일은 5월 23일이에요.
je saeng-ireun owol isipsamirieyo
My birthday is on May 23rd.

3. Attached to a verb stem, '거/것' is the future tense marker. '거' is used with the '~예요' sentence ending, and '것' is used with the '~입니다' sentence ending. These variations are related to pronunciation.

학교에 갈 거예요. : I will go to school.

집에 갈 거예요. (갈 것입니다.)
jibe gal geoyeyo
I will go home.

집에 있을 거예요. (있을 것입니다.)
jibe isseul geoyeyo
I will be home.

공부를 할 거예요. (할 것입니다.)
gongbureul hal geoyeyo
I will study.

저녁을 먹을 거예요. (먹을 것입니다.)
jeonyeogeul meogeul geoyeyo
I will have dinner.

④ The question word '언제' is used to ask about a date, meaning 'when'.

생일은 언제예요? : When is your birthday?

파티는 언제예요?
patineun eonjeyeyo
When is your party?

방학은 언제예요?
banghageun eonjeyeyo
When is your vacation?

⑤ Attached after a noun, postposition '~에' is used to indicate a place, a time and a direction. On the other hand, '~에서' is used to indicate a place only.

도서관에서 in/at a library
doseogwaneseo

학교에 at school, to school
hakgyoe

집에 at home
jibe

7시에 at 7 o'clock
ilgopsie

⑥ Construction '우리 ~ Verb stem + 요' is used to suggest an idea, meaning 'let's' in English.

우리 ~ Verb stem + **요** : Let's ~

우리 생일 파티해요.
uri saeng-il patihaeyo
Let's have a birthday party.

우리 학교에 가요.
uri hakgyoe gayo
Let's go to school.

우리 집에 가요.
uri jibe gayo
Let's go home.

우리 텔레비전 봐요.
uri tellebijyeon bwayo
Let's watch the television program.

Exercises

1 Form a question and answer using each word as shown in the example. (1)~(2)

(1)

Example

Q : 오늘은 무슨 요일입니까? (화요일) What day is it today?
A : 오늘은 화요일입니다. Today is Tuesday.

① 월요일 Monday ② 수요일 Wednesday
③ 일요일 Sunday ④ 토요일 Saturday
⑤ 금요일 Friday

(2)

Example

Q : 내일은 어디에 갈 거예요? (학교) Where are you going tomorrow?
A : 학교에 갈 거예요. I'm going to school.

① 친구 집 my friend's house ② 도서관 library
③ 회사 company/work ④ 교회 church
⑤ 시장 market

2 Complete the following dialog using each date below.

Example

Q : 생일은 언제예요? When is your birthday?
A : 제 생일은 ( )이에요. My birthday is ....

(1) 5월 23일 (2) 1월 12일 (3) 2월 5일 (4) 12월 31일
(5) 3월 7일 (6) 10월 17일 (7) 8월 28일

3 Change the following sentences into the negative form.

(1) 학교에 가다 go to school
(2) 친구를 만나다 meet friends

(3) 주스를 마시다 drink some juice
(4) 한국어를 배우다 study the Korean language

4 Make suggestion sentences using the following structure.

Exemple
우리 ~ Verb stem + 요

(1) 생일 파티하다 have a birthday party
(2) 공부하다 study
(3) 학교에 가다 go to school
(4) 도서관에 가다 go to the library
(5) 집에 있다 be home

Reading Practice

(1) 어제는 집에서 공부를 했어요.
Yesterday I studied at home.

(2) 오늘은 수요일입니다.
Today is Wednesday.

(3) 주말에는 무엇을 합니까?
What do you do on weekends?

(4) 생일이 내일이에요.
My birthday is tomorrow.

(5) 모레 아침 10시에 우리 집에 오세요.
Please come to my house the day after tomorrow at 10 o'clock.

제 7 과

몇 개 있어요? How Many Do You Have?

Key Sentences

1. 펜이 몇 개 있어요? How many pens do you have?
   peni myeot gae isseoyo
2. 친구가 몇 명 있어요? How many friends do you have?
   chin-guga myeot myeong isseoyo

Dialogs

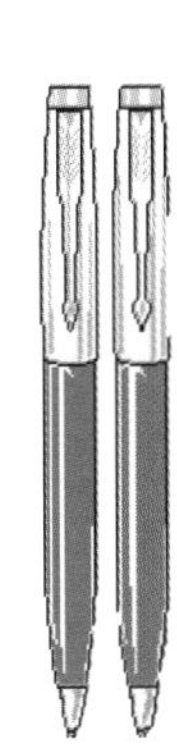

Dialog 1

인 수: 펜을 안 가져왔어요.
peneul an gajyeowasseoyo
I didn't bring a pen.

펜이 몇 개 있어요?
peni myeot gae isseoyo
How many pens do you have?

요시코: 두 자루 있어요. 빌려 드릴까요?
du jaru isseoyo billyeo deurilkkayo
I have two. Shall I lend you a pen?

인 수: 한 개 빌려 주세요.
han gae billyeo juseyo
Please, lend me a pen.

요시코: 여기 있어요. 파란색이에요. Here it is. It's blue.
yeogi isseoyo paransaekieyo

인 수: 고마워요. Thank you.
gomawoyo

Dialog 2

수 미: 요시코 씨, 한국인 친구가 몇 명 있어요?
yosiko ssi han-gugin chin-guga myeot myeong isseoyo
Yosiko, how many Korean friends do you have?

요시코: 다섯 명 있어요.
daseot myeong isseoyo
I have five.

수　미: 남자 친구도 있어요?
namja chin-gudo isseoyo
Do you also have any male friends?

요시코: 네, 남자 친구도 두 명 있어요.
ne namja chin-gudo du myeong isseoyo
Yes, I also have two male friends.

여자 친구는 세 명이에요.
yeoja chin-guneun se myeong-ieyo
I have three female friends.

수　미: 친구가 많아서 좋겠어요.
chin-guga manaseo jokesseoyo
It is good that you have many friends.

Vocabulary and Phrases

- 몇 개　how many (things)
- 안　not
- 좋겠어요　will be good
- 여기　here
- 파란색　blue
- 한국인　Korean
- 친구　friend
- 여자 친구　female friend
- 다섯 명　five people
- 빌려 주다/빌려 드리다　to lend
- 펜　pen
- 가져오다　to bring
- 빌려 주세요　to lend
- 여기 있어요　here it is
- 고마워요　thank you
- 몇 명　how many (people)
- 남자 친구　male friend
- 많다　many/much/a lot
- 두 명　two people

Word Drills

Numbers : The second column is the sino-Korean numbers and the third column is the pure Korean numbers.

1	일 il	하나(한) hana(han)	8	팔 pal	여덟 yeodeol
2	이 i	둘 (두) dul(du)	9	구 gu	아홉 ahop
3	삼 sam	셋 (세) set(se)	10	십 sip	열 yeol
4	사 sa	넷 (네) net(ne)	100	백 baek	백 baek
5	오 o	다섯 daseot	1,000	천 cheon	천 cheon
6	육 yuk	여섯 yeoseot	10,000	만 man	만 man
7	칠 chil	일곱 ilgop			

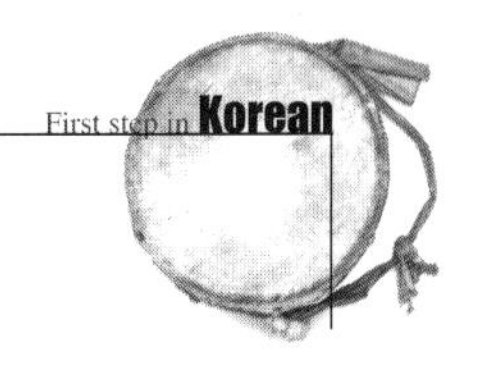

Structures and Expressions

① When you count things, use the numeral classifier '개' after '몇'.

몇 개 있어요? : How many do you have?

펜이 몇 개 있어요?
peni myeot gae isseoyo
How many pens do you have?

연필이 몇 개 있어요?
yeonpiri myeot gae isseoyo
How many pencils do you have?

② '~ㄹ까요?' is the polite informal style of asking a question from the first person's point of view, whose corresponding structure in English is, 'Shall I / Shall we...?'

~ㄹ까요? : Shall I / Shall we...?

펜을 빌려 드릴까요?
peneul billyeo deurilkkayo
Shall I lend you a pen?

학교에 갈까요?
hakgyoe galkkayo
Shall we go to school?

③ When you count people, use the numeral classifier '명' after '몇'.

몇 명 있어요? : How many (friends) do you have?

친구가 몇 명 있어요?
chin-guga myeot myeong isseoyo
How many friends do you have?

학생이 몇 명 있어요?
haksaeng-i myeot myeong isseoyo
How many students do you have?

④ When you need to borrow something from someone, use the expression '빌려 주세요'.

빌려 주세요. : Would you lend me ~?

펜 빌려 주세요.
pen billyeo juseyo
Please lend me a pen.

연필 빌려 주세요.
yeonpil billyeo juseyo
Please lend me a pencil.

돈 빌려 주세요.
don billyeo juseyo
Please lend me some money.

책 빌려 주세요.
chaek billyeo juseyo
Please lend me a book.

⑤ '안' is used to negate a verb or an adjective, preceded by the verb or the adjective.

안 + verb : not + verb
안 + adjective : not + adjective

안 가져왔어요.
an gajyeowasseoyo
I didn't bring it.

안 먹었어요.
an meogeosseoyo
I didn't eat it.

안 예뻐요.
an yeppeoyo
(She is) not pretty.

⑥ The causal connective '~아서/~어서' has the meaning 'because', attached after a verb or an adjective. '서' may be deleted without changing the meaning.

많 + **아(서)** : Because you have many...

친구가 많아(서) 좋겠어요.
chin-guga mana(seo) jokesseoyo
It will be good because you have many friends.

펜을 빌려서 좋겠어요.
peneul billyeoseo jokesseoyo
It will be good because you have borrowed a pen.

⑦ The future tense marker '~겠' is used to indicate the future tense, attached after a verb stem or an adjective.

좋겠어요. : will be good

좋겠어요.
jokesseoyo
(It) will be good.

가겠어요.
gagesseoyo
(I) will go.

공부하겠어요.
gongbuhagesseoyo
(I) will study.

Exercises

1 Complete the following dialogs using each word in the boxes.

(1) Question : 펜이 몇 개 있어요? How many pens do you have?

Answer : 펜이 한 개 있어요.

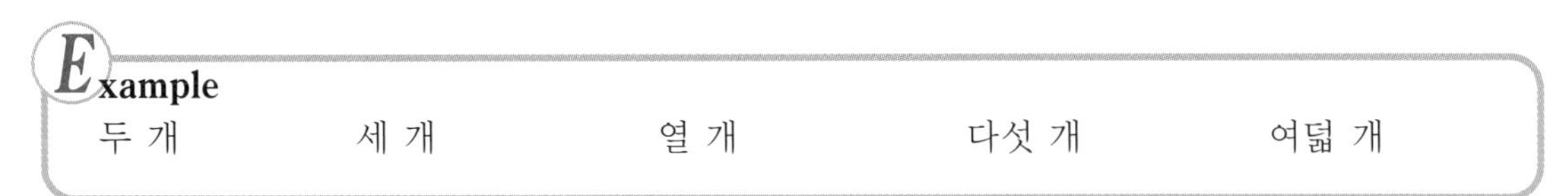

(2) Question : 친구가 몇 명 있어요? How many friends do you have?

Answer : 저는 친구가 네 명 있어요.

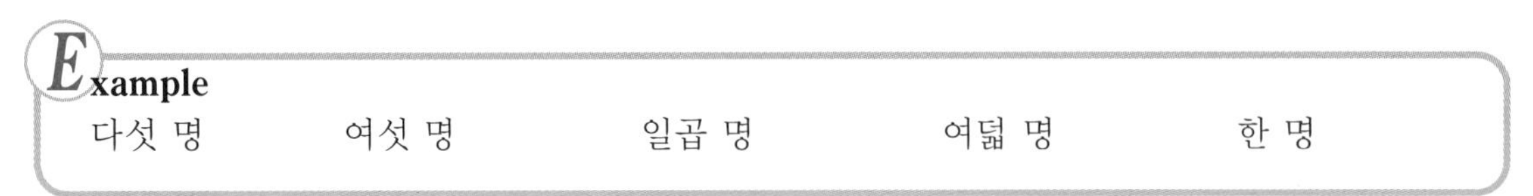

Example
다섯 명
여섯 명
일곱 명
여덟 명
한 명

(3) 저에게 책을(를) 빌려 주세요. Please lend me a book.

2 Change the following sentences into question form.

(1) 친구가 있다. I have friends.

→ ______________________

(2) 봄을 좋아하다. I like spring.

→ ______________________

(3) 비가 오다. It is raining.

→ ______________________

(4) 날씨가 흐리다. It is cloudy.

→ ______________________

(5) 우산을 가져오다. I have brought an umbrella.

→ ______________________

3 Using '안', change the following sentences into the negative form.

(1) 가져왔어요? Did you bring it?

(2) 점심을 먹었어요. I ate lunch.

(3) 책을 샀어요. I bought the book.

(4) 갈 거예요? Will you go?

(5) 시원해요. It's cool.

Reading Practice

(1) 펜 한 개 빌려 주세요.
Please lend me a pen.

(2) 파란색 펜이 몇 개 있어요?
How many blue pens do you have?

(3) 한국인 친구가 몇 명 있어요?
How many Korean friends do you have?

(4) 남자 친구가 다섯 명 있어요.
I have five male friends.

(5) 공책을 안 가져왔어요.
I didn't bring a notebook.

제 8 과
Lesson 8

얼마입니까? How Much Is It?

Key Sentences

1. 이것은 얼마입니까? How much are they?/How much is it?
   igeoseun eolmaimnikka
2. 모두 이천팔백 원입니다. Altogether, it's 2,800 won.
   modu icheonpalbaek wonimnida

Dialogs

Dialog 1

주　인: 어서 오세요. Welcome.
eoseo oseyo

요시코: 바나나는 백 그램에 얼마입니까?
banananeun baek graeme eolmaimnikka
How much are bananas per 100g?

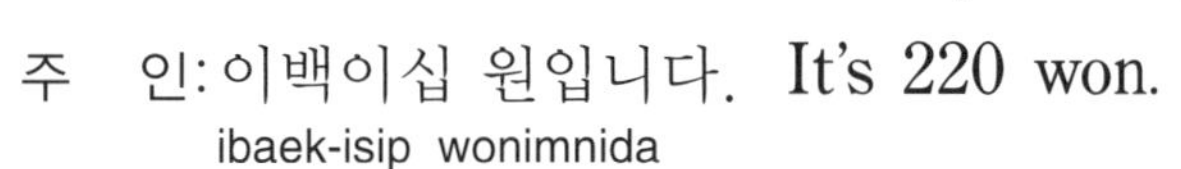

주　인: 이백이십 원입니다. It's 220 won.
ibaek-isip wonimnida

요시코: 이 킬로그램 주세요. Please give me 2kg.
ikillograem juseyo.

주　인: 여기 있습니다. Here they are.
yeogi itseumnida

모두 사천사백 원입니다. It's 4,400 won in total.
modu sacheonsabaek wonimnida

Dialog 2

요시코: 오이는 얼마입니까? How much are the cucumbers?
oineun eolmaimnikka

주　인: 세 개에 천백 원입니다. It's 1,100 won for three.
se gae-e cheonbaek wonimnida

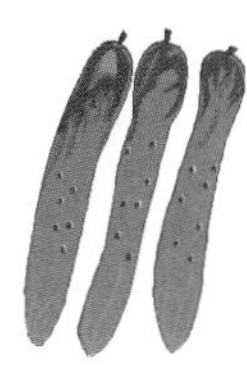

요시코: 토마토는 얼마입니까?
tomatoneun eolmaimnikka
How much are the tomatoes?

주　인: 백 그램에 이백육십 원입니다.
baek graeme ibaek-yuksip wonimnida
It's 260 won per 100g.

요시코: 오이 세 개와 토마토 1킬로그램 주세요.
oi se gaewa tomato ilkillograem juseyo
Please give me three cucumbers and 1kg of tomatoes.

주　인: 모두 삼천칠백 원입니다.
modu samcheonchilbaek wonimnida
It's 3,700 won altogether.

Vocabulary and Phrases

- 어서 오세요　welcome
- 얼마입니까?　how much
- 이백이십 원　220 won
- 여기 있습니다　here it is
- 사천사백 원　4,400 won
- 세 개에　for 3
- 토마토　tomato
- ~와/과　and
- 바나나　banana
- 백 그램에　per 100g
- 이 킬로그램　2kg
- 모두　altogether
- 오이　cucumber
- 천백 원　1,100 won
- 이백육십 원　260 won
- 삼천칠백 원　3,700 won

Word Drills

Fruits

사과
sagwa
apple

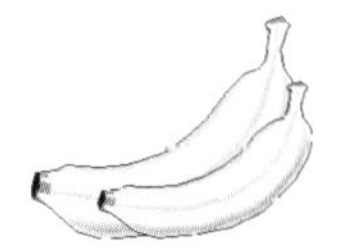
바나나
banana
banana

파인애플
painaepeul
pineapple

배
bae
pear

포도
podo
grape

수박
subak
watermelon

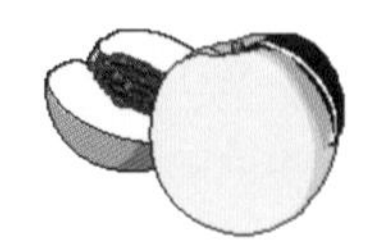
복숭아
boksunga
peach

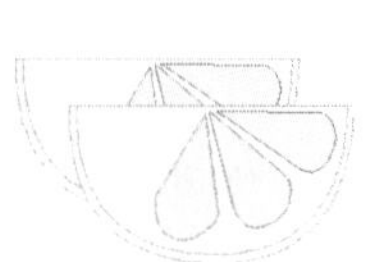
오렌지
orenji
orange

감
gam
persimmon

레몬
remon
lemon

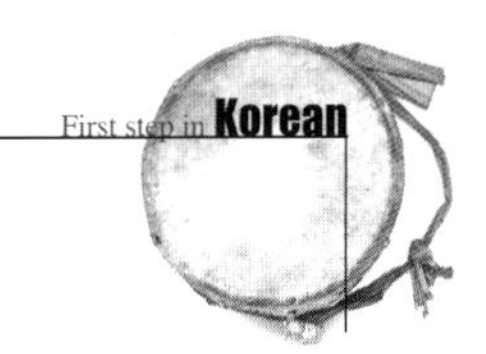

Vegetables

오이 cucumber
oi

호박 pumpkin
hobak

무 radish
mu

시금치 spinach
sigeumchi

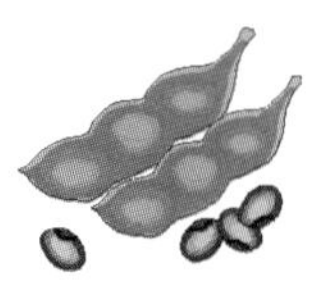

콩 bean
kong

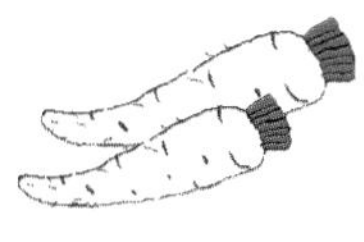

당근 carrot
danggeun

배추 chinese cabbage
baechu

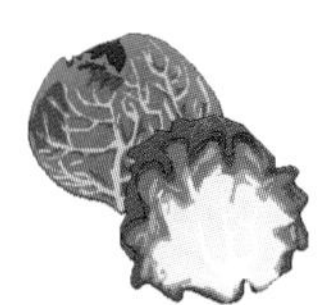

양배추 cabbage
yangbaechu

고추 pepper
gochu

파 green onion
pa

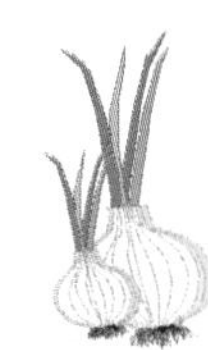

양파 onion
yangpa

마늘 garlic
maneul

Money Denomination

십 원	10 won [sip won]	천 원	1,000 won [cheon won]
오십 원	50 won [osip won]	오천 원	5,000 won [ocheon won]
백 원	100 won [baek won]	만 원	10,000 won [man won]
오백 원	500 won [obaek won]		

Structures and Expressions

1. When you ask about the price, use the expression '얼마입니까?'.

얼마입니까? : How much is it?

바나나 100g에 얼마입니까?
banana baekgeuraeme eolmaimnikka
How much are the bananas per 100g?

토마토 100g에 얼마입니까?
tomato baekgeuraeme eolmaimnikka
How much are the tomatoes per 100g?

② When you buy something, use the expression '주세요'. Generally '주세요' means 'give me something'. This expression is widely used for buying things, ordering things (L9), and asking favors, as you will see in the following chapters.

~ 주세요. : Please give me ~.

사과를 세 개 주세요.
sagwareul se gae juseyo
Please give me three apples.

바나나를 주세요.
bananareul juseyo
Please give me some bananas.

③ Use the expression '모두', to express a total amount or number.

모두 삼천칠백 원입니다. : The total comes to 3,700 won.

모두 사천사백 원입니다.
modu sacheonsabaek wonimnida
It is 4,400 won in total.

모두 천오십 원입니다.
modu cheon-osip wonimnida
It is 1,050 won in total.

④ '~에' in '백 그램에' corresponds to 'per' in English.

100g에 220 원 : 220 won per 100g
1kg에 2,600 원 : 2,600 won per 1kg

100g에 150 원입니다.
baekgeuraeme baek-osip wonimnida
It is 150 won per 100g.

1kg에 1,500 원입니다.
ilkillograeme cheon-obaek wonimnida
It is 1,500 won per 1kg.

⑤ '~와/과' is used to conjoin nouns like 'and' in English. '~와' is attached after a noun which ends with a vowel, and '~과' is attached after a noun which ends with a consonant.

오이 세 개와 토마토 두 개 : three cucumbers and two tomatoes

바나나와 사과
bananawa sagwa
bananas and apples

감자 1kg과 당근 600g
gamja ilkillograemgwa dang-geun yukbaekgraem
1kg of potatoes and 600g of carrots

Exercises

1 Complete the following sentences using each word in the box. (1)~(2).

(1) (　　　　　)은(는) 100g에 얼마입니까?

How much is 100g of (　　　　　)?

Example

바나나　　오렌지　　딸기　　자두　　앵두　　사과

(2) (　　　　　)은(는) 얼마입니까?

How much are the (　　　　　)?

Example

토마토　　당근　　오이　　고추　　마늘

2 Practice the following expressions using words in the boxes.

100g 두 개 세 개 1kg 한 근	에	이천 원 이천오백 원 천 원 오천 원 삼천오백 원	입니다.

note Note that '근' is a weight unit used in Korea. One '근' is approximately 375g and 600g for a small '근' and a big '근' respectively.

3 Please read the following prices.

(1) 230 원　　(2) 12,300 원　　(3) 7,560 원

(4) 354,000 원　　(5) 90 원

4 Write down the expression when you total the price.

(1) (　　　　　) 5,600 원입니다.　　(2) (　　　　　) 7,200 원입니다.

(3) (　　　　　) 1,800 원입니다.

Reading Practice

(1) 사과는 얼마예요?
How much are the apples?

(2) 감은 얼마예요?
How much are the persimmons?

(3) 사과 한 봉지에 삼천육백 원입니다.
It's 3,600 won for an apple bag.

(4) 오렌지 한 개에 오백 원이에요.
It's 500 won per orange.

(5) 토마토 2kg 주세요.
Please give me 2kg of tomatoes.

제 9 과

Lesson 9

비빔밥 한 그릇 주세요.
Please Give Me One Bibimbap.

Key Sentences

1. 무엇을 드시겠습니까? — What would you like to have?
   mueoseul deusigesseumnikka
2. 비빔밥 한 그릇 주세요. — I will have an order of Bibimbap.
   bibimbap han geureut juseyo

Dialogs

Dialog 1

종업원: 무엇을 드시겠습니까? What would you like to have?
mueoseul deusigesseumnikka

메뉴에 불고기, 비빔밥, 설렁탕이 있어요.
menyue bulgogi bibimbap seolleongtang-i isseoyo
We have Bulgogi, Bibimbap, and Seolleongtang on the menu.

인 수: 저는 비빔밥 한 그릇 주세요.
jeoneun bibimbap han geureut juseyo
Please give me an order of Bibimbap.

요시코: 저는 설렁탕을 먹을래요. I will have Seolleongtang.
jeoneun seolleongtang-eul meogeullaeyo

종업원: 잠시만 기다리세요.
jamsiman gidariseyo
Please wait a minute.

여기 설렁탕 한 그릇, 비빔밥 한 그릇입니다.
yeogi seolleongtang han geureut bibimbap han geureut-imnida
Here is one Bibimbap and one Seolleongtang.

요시코: (다 먹고 난 후) 설렁탕이 맛있어요.
seolleongtang-i masisseoyo
Seolleongtang is tasty.

Dialog 2

요시코: 이 자동판매기는 어떻게 사용해요?
i jadongpanmaegineun eotteoke sayonghaeyo
How do I use this vending machine?

인 수: 100원짜리 동전을 세 개 넣으세요.
baekwonjjari dongjeoneul se gae neoeuseyo
Please insert three 100 won coins,

그리고 버튼을 누르세요. and press a button.
geurigo beoteuneul nureuseyo

요시코: 어느 것을 누를까요?
eoneu geoseul nureulkkayo
Which button should I press?

밀크 커피, 설탕 커피, 블랙 커피가 있어요.
milk keopi seoltang keopi beullaek keopiga isseoyo
There is coffee with milk, coffee with sugar, and black coffee.

인 수: 저는 밀크 커피 마실게요. I will drink coffee with milk.
jeoneun milk keopi masilgeyo

Vocabulary and Phrases

- ~드시겠습니까? Would you like to have ~?
- 비빔밥 Bibimbap
- 불고기 Bulgogi
- 설렁탕 Seolleongtang
- 메뉴 menu
- 잠시 기다려요 wait a minute
- 맛있다 to be delicious/tasty
- 이 this
- 자동판매기 vending machine
- 어떻게 how
- 사용하다 to use
- 100원 짜리 100 won piece coin
- 동전 coin
- 넣다 to insert
- 그리고 and
- 버튼 button
- 누르다 to push
- 어느 것 which one
- 밀크 커피 coffee with milk
- 설탕 커피 coffee with sugar
- 블랙 커피 black coffee
- 마시다 to drink
- 마실게요 will drink

Word Drills

Korean food

김치 (kimchi)

포기김치, 물김치, 깍두기, 보쌈김치, 총각김치, 오이소박이, 파김치, 부추김치, 깻잎김치

밥 (steamed rice)

쌀밥, 보리밥, 잡곡밥, 팥밥, 차조밥

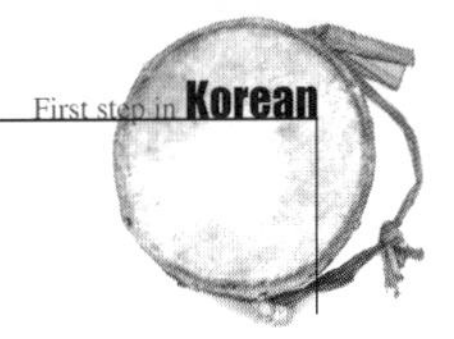

나물 (seasoned vegetables [greens])

시금치, 콩나물, 고사리, 숙주나물, 파래무침, 도라지무침, 오이무침, 호박볶음, 무채나물

생선 (fish)

조기, 옥돔, 참치, 꽁치, 갈치, 고등어, 가자미, 대구, 명태

전 (panfried food; grilled food)

고기산적, 녹두지짐, 파전, 깻잎전, 호박전, 감자전

찌개 (stew)

된장찌개, 김치찌개, 참치찌개, 두부찌개, 비지찌개, 동태찌개, 버섯전골, 오징어전골

국 (soup)

미역국, 북어국, 쇠고기국, 감자국, 무국, 시금치된장국, 배추된장국, 콩나물국, 육개장, 떡국, 만두국, 삼계탕

Structures and Expressions

1. When you order food in a restaurant, use '인 분' after sino-Korean numbering, or you can use the numeral classifier '그릇' after pure Korean numbering.

(1) 비빔밥 ________ 그릇 : '한 그릇' is one order.
bibimbap geureut

한	세	다섯	일곱	열

(2) 불고기 ________ 인분 : '일 인 분' is one order.
bulgogi inbun

일	이	육	구	십

2. Use the expression '드시겠습니까?' to ask about someone's preference. The expression is analyzed as '드시＋겠＋습니까?'. '드시다' is an honorific word of '먹다' (eat). '시' is the honorific marker, '겠' is the future tense marker, and '습니까?' is the polite formal question ending.

________ **을(를) 드시겠습니까?** : Would you like to have (   )?

비빔밥 bibimbap	불고기 bulgogi	우동 udong	국수 guksu	수제비 sujebi	떡국 tteokguk

③ '먹을래요?' is the polite informal style of asking a question, analyzed as '먹다 (eat) + 으 + ㄹ래요?'. '~ㄹ래요?' asks about the listener's intention. '으' is inserted for the ease of pronunciation, because the verb stem '먹' ends with a consonant. The same analysis applies to '마실래요?', as in '마시다 (drink) + ㄹ래요?'. Unlike '먹을래요?', the verb stem in this word ends with a vowel, so that the vowel insertion is not necessary, resulting in '마실래요?'. As mentioned before, note that the same sentence ending works for a statement, not a question, with a falling intonation. In that case, '~ㄹ래요?' means the speaker's will or intention.

________ **을(를) 먹을래요?** : Would you like to have ( )?
________ **을(를) 마실래요?** : Would you like to drink ( )?

라면 ramyeon	피자 pija	김밥 gimbap	햄버거 haembeogeo	국수 guksu
커피 keopi	콜라 kolla	사이다 saida	주스 juseu	

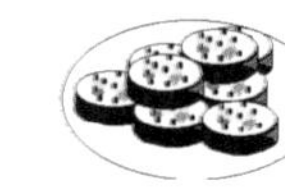
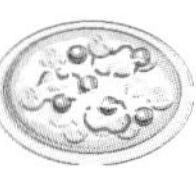

④ To order food in a restaurant, use the expression '주세요'. Recall that the same expression was used for buying things. (L8)

________ **주세요.** : Please give me ( ).

삼계탕 일인 분 samgyetang ilinbun	한정식 이인 분 hanjeongsik i-inbun	불고기 육인 분 bulgogi yuk-inbun
설렁탕 한 그릇 seolleongtang han geureut	자장면 세 그릇 jajangmyeon se geureut	

⑤ '어떻게' is a question word meaning 'how', asking about a way of doing things.

어떻게 : how

어떻게 사용해요? eotteoke sayonghaeyo How do I use it?	어떻게 가요? eotteoke gayo How do I get there?

⑥ The sentence ending '마실게요' is used with a verb to indicate an intention of a first person subject.

~(으)ㄹ게요. : will do

밀크 커피 마실게요.
milk keopi masilgeyo
I will drink coffee with milk.

공부할게요.
gongbuhalgeyo
I will study.

불고기 먹을게요.
bulgogi meogeulgeyo
I will eat Bulgogi.

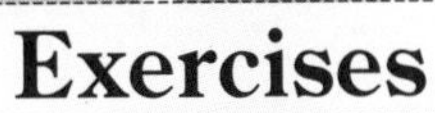

Exercises

1 Provide an appropriate answer for the question, using each word in parenthesis.

Question
Q : 무엇을 드시겠습니까? What would you like to have?

(1) ________ 먹을래요. (불고기)　(2) ________ 먹을래요. (설렁탕)
(3) ________ 먹을래요. (자장면)　(4) ________ 먹을래요. (우동)

2 Provide questions to ask if it is tasty.

(1) 비빔밥이 ________?　(2) 불고기가 ________?
(3) 설렁탕이 ________?　(4) 자장면이 ________?
(5) 물냉면이 ________?　(6) 된장찌개가 ________?

3 Place an order using words in the box.

김밥	생선초밥	짬뽕	갈비	비빔냉면
만두국	떡만두국	칼국수	버섯전골	오징어전골

(1) Using '그릇', place an order.

Example
칼국수 한 그릇 주세요. Give me one 칼국수, please.

① ________ 주세요.　② ________ 주세요.
③ ________ 주세요.　④ ________ 주세요.
⑤ ________ 주세요.

(2) Using '~인 분', place an order.

Example

만두 이 인 분 주세요. Give me two orders of 만두, please.

① ____________ 주세요. ② ____________ 주세요.

③ ____________ 주세요. ④ ____________ 주세요.

⑤ ____________ 주세요.

4 Using the words in exercise **3**, complete the following sentences.

(1) ____________ 이(가) 맛있어요. (2) ____________ 이(가) 맛없어요.

(3) ____________ 이(가) 맛있어요. (4) ____________ 이(가) 맛없어요.

(5) ____________ 이(가) 맛있어요. (6) ____________ 이(가) 맛없어요.

(7) ____________ 이(가) 맛있어요. (8) ____________ 이(가) 맛없어요.

5 Complete the following sentences using words in the box.

Example

밀크 커피 설탕 커피 블랙 커피 율무차 코코아 유자차

▸ Would you like to have (   )?

(1) ____________ 마실래요? (2) ____________ 마실래요?

(3) ____________ 마실래요? (4) ____________ 마실래요?

(5) ____________ 마실래요? (6) ____________ 마실래요?

Reading Practice

(1) 무엇을 드시겠습니까? What would you like to have?

(2) 자장면 한 그릇 주세요. Please give me one order of jajangmyeon.

(3) 100원짜리 동전을 다섯 개 넣으세요. Please insert five 100 won coins.

(4) 저는 블랙 커피 마실게요. I will drink black coffee.

(5) 우동 두 그릇 주세요. Please give me two orders of udong.

제 10 과

Lesson 10

여보세요? Hello?

Key Sentences

1. 여보세요? Hello?
   yeoboseyo
2. 수미 씨 있어요? Is Sumi there?
   sumi ssi isseoyo

Dialogs

Dialog 1

요시코: 여보세요? 인수 씨 있어요?
yeoboseyo insu ssi isseoyo
Hello? Is Insu there?

인 수: 저예요. 요시코 씨. Yosiko, this is he.
jeoyeyo yosiko ssi

요시코: 몇 시에 만날까요?
myeot sie mannalkkayo
What time shall we meet?

인 수: 2시에 만나요. Let's meet at 2 o'clock.
dusie mannayo

요시코: 어디에서 만날까요? Where shall we meet?
eodieseo mannalkkayo

인 수: 이태원 맥도날드에서 만나요.
itaewon maekdonaldeu-eseo mannayo
Let's meet at McDonald's in Itaewon.

Dialog 2

요시코: 여보세요? Hello?
yeoboseyo

소 라: 누구세요? Who is this?
nuguseyo

요시코: 저는 요시코예요. This is Yosiko.
jeoneun yosikoyeyo

소　라: 누구 찾으세요? Who are you looking for?
nugu chajeuseyo

요시코: 인수 씨를 찾습니다.
insu ssireul chasseumnida
I'm looking for Insu.

소　라: 지금 여기 안 계십니다.
jigeum yeogi an gyesimnida
He is not here now.

요시코: 요시코가 전화했다고 전해 주세요.
yosikoga jeonhwahaetdago jeonhae juseyo
Please tell him that Yosiko called.

Vocabulary and Phrases

- ~씨 Ms. or Mr.
- 있어요? Is(Are) there...?
- 없어요? Isn't(Aren't) there...?
- 저예요 it is me
- 지금 now
- 여기 here
- 안 not
- 2시 2 o'clock
- 어디에서 where
- 이태원 Itaewon
- 맥도날드 McDonald's
- 여보세요? hello (telephone)
- 누구 who
- (누구를) 찾으세요? to look for
- 몇 시 What time?
- 만날까요? Shall we meet?
- 만나다 to see, to meet
- 계십니다 (she) is here
- 안 계십니다 (she) is not here
- 전화했다고 called
- 전해 주세요 please tell
- 전화 telephone

Word Drills

Telling the time

- 한 시 1:00 hansi
- 두 시 2:00 dusi
- 세 시 3:00 sesi
- 네 시 4:00 nesi
- 다섯 시 5:00 daseotsi
- 한 시 반 1:30 hansi ban
- 두 시 반 2:30 dusi ban
- 세 시 반 3:30 sesi ban
- 네 시 반 4:30 nesi ban
- 한 시 십 분 1:10 hansi sipbun
- 두 시 이십 분 2:20 dusi isipbun
- 세 시 사십 분 3:40 sesi sasipbun
- 네 시 십 분 전 3:50 nesi sipbun jeon
- 다섯 시 십오 분 전 4:45 daseotsi sipobun jeon

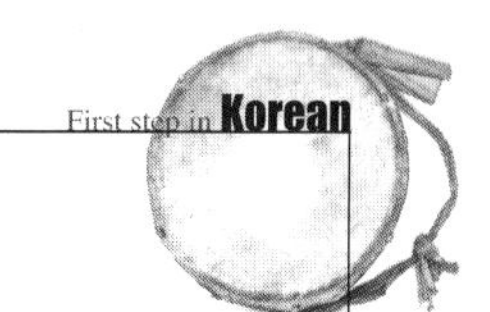

세 시 3:00
sesi

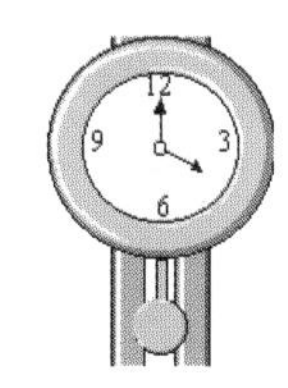

네 시 4:00
nesi

열두 시 오십오 분 12:55
yeoldusi osipobun
한 시 오 분 전
hansi obun jeon

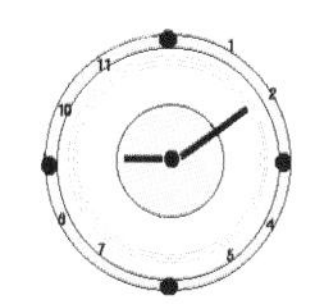

아홉 시 십 분 9:10
ahopsi sipbun

여섯 시 오십 분 6:50
yeoseosi osipbun
일곱 시 십 분 전
ilgopsi sipbun jeon

두 시 오십오 분 2:55
dusi osipobun
세 시 오 분 전
sesi obun jeon

한 시 사십오 분 1:45
hansi sasipobun

다섯 시 5:00
daseotsi

열두 시 사십 분 12:40
yeoldusi sasipbun

열 시 반 10:30
yeolsi ban
열 시 삼십 분
yeolsi samsipbun

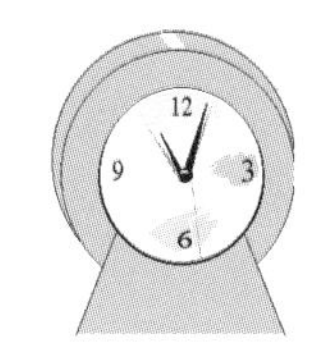

열한 시 오 분 11:05
yeolhansi obun

Types of question words

누구 (who)	**무엇** (what)	**어디** (where)	**언제** (when)
어느 것 (which)	**어떻게** (how)	**왜** (why)	

누구를 좋아합니까?
nugureul joahamnikka
Who do you like?

무엇을 합니까?
mueoseul hamnikka
What do you do?

어디에 갑니까?
eodie gamnikka
Where are you going?

언제 갑니까?
eonje gamnikka
When do you go?

어느 것을 좋아합니까?
eoneu geoseul joahamnikka
Which one do you like?

어떻게 사용합니까?
eotteoke sayonghamnikka
How do I use it?

Structures and Expressions

① When you make a phone call, use the expression '여보세요?' to start a conversation.

여보세요? : Hello?

② When you ask if the person you are calling is available to speak, use the expression '있어요?'. The honorific word for '있어요?' is '계세요?'. '있어요?' is used for friends or for close relationships and '계세요?' is used for people who are higher in social status or older or in formal relationship.

_________ **있어요? / 계세요?** : Is there _________ ?

수미 씨	헨리 씨	소라 씨	앤디 씨	영주 씨	존 씨
사장님	과장님	목사님	원장님	선생님	신부님

③ When you don't know the person who is calling, ask who (he or she) is by using the expression '누구세요?'. When you don't know who the person is calling, use the expression '누구 찾으세요?'.

누구세요? : Who is this? **누구(를) 찾으세요?** : Who are you looking for?

④ The question ending '~(으)ㄹ까요?' asks about the listener's intention.

_________ **만날까요?** : Shall I see you _________?

두 시에	네 시에	다섯 시에	일곱 시에
du sie	ne sie	daseot sie	ilgop sie
at two o'clock	at four o'clock	at five o'clock	at seven o'clock

⑤ For the polite informal statement, attach '~요' after verb stems. And '~에서' is a postposition positioned after a noun.

_________ **에서 만나요.** : Let's meet at _________.

맥도날드	버거킹	웬디스	지하철역
maekdonaldeu	beogeoking	wendis	jihacheolyeok
McDonald's	Burger King	Wendy's	subway station

⑥ When you want to leave a message, use the expression '~고 전해 주세요' after making your statement. '~고' is a complementizer leading a clause, corresponding to 'that' in English.

~고 전해 주세요 : Please tell him that ~

전화했다고 전해 주세요. Please tell him that I called.
jeonhwahaetdago jeonhae juseyo

찾는다고 전해 주세요. Please tell him that I am looking for him.
channeundago jeonhae juseyo

Note that the past tense marker '~었' is attached to the verb stem, providing a contracted form '전화했다'. The present tense marker '~는' is attached to the verb stem, resulting in '찾는다'.

Exercises

1 Using each name in parenthesis, complete the following dialog.

Example
여보세요? 수미 씨 있어요? : Hello? Is Sumi there?

(1) ______? ______ 있어요?(요시코) (2) ______? ______ 있어요?(재헌)

(3) ______? ______ 있어요?(사무엘) (4) ______? ______ 있어요?(푸휘)

2 Provide the answers to the following question relating to the clauses in parenthesis.

Example
여보세요? (your name) 씨 있어요?

Answer 1 : ____________ (You know the person who's calling.)
Answer 2 : ____________ (You don't know the person who's calling.)

3 Insert appropriate words in the blanks.

(1) ________에 만날까요? (Ask about the time.)

(2) ________에 만나요. (Answer a certain time.)

(3) ________에서 만날까요? (Ask what place.)

(4) ________에서 만나요. (Answer with a place.)

4 Rewrite the sentences using the honorific words.

(1) 나는 인수예요. → ________. I'm Insu.

(2) 그녀는 요시코예요. → ________. She's Yosiko.

(3) 우리는 학생이에요. → ________. We are students.

(4) 그들은 선생님이에요. → ________. They are teachers.

(5) 이 사람은 누구예요? → ________. Who is this person?

(6) 나는 이사를 만났어요. → ________. I met the president of a company.

(7) 나는 전무를 만났어요. → ________. I met a managing director.

(8) 나는 부장을 만났어요. → ________. I met the head of a department.

(9) 나는 과장을 만났어요. → ________. I met the head of a section.

Reading Practice

(1) 여보세요? 114입니까?
Hello? Is this 114?

(2) 인수 씨 있어요?
Is Insu there?

(3) 요시코가 전화했다고 전해 주세요.
Please tell him that Yosiko called.

(4) 몇 시에 어디에서 만날까요?
When and where shall we meet?

(5) 인수 씨는 지금 여기 안 계십니다.
Insu is not here now.

제 11 과
Lesson 11

이태원은 어떻게 가요?
How Do I Get to Itaewon?

Key Sentences

1. 이태원은 어떻게 가요? — How do I get to Itaewon?
   itaewoneun eotteoke gayo
2. 지하철을 타세요. — Take the subway.
   jihacheoreul taseyo

Dialogs

Dialog 1

존 : 이태원은 어떻게 가요?
itaewoneun eotteoke gayo
How do I get to Itaewon?

유미: 지하철 6호선을 타세요.
jihacheol yukhoseoneul taseyo
Take the line 6 subway.

그리고, 이태원 역에서 내리세요.
geurigo itaewon yeogeseo naeriseyo
And get off at 이태원 station.

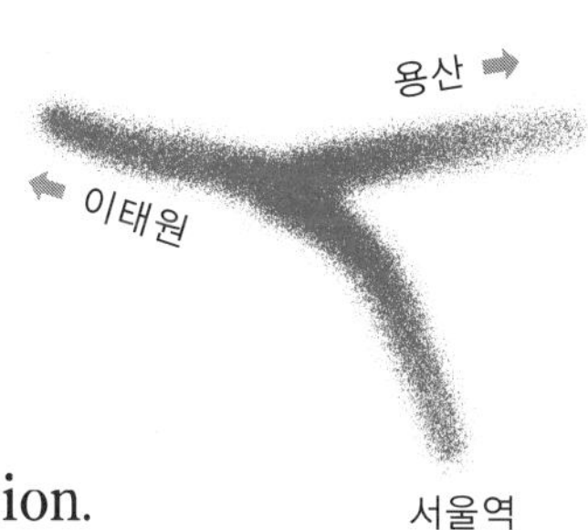

존 : 맥도날드는 어떻게 가요?
maekdonaldneun eotteoke gayo
How do I get to McDonald's?

유미: 지하철 역에서 걸어서 가세요.
jihacheol yeogeseo georeoseo gaseyo
You can walk from the subway station.

존 : 걸어서 얼마나 걸려요?
georeoseo eolmana geollyeoyo
How long does it take on foot?

유미: 금방이에요.
geumbangieyo
It doesn't take long.

Dialog 2

존 : 이태원 역 한 장 주세요.
itaewon-yeok hanjang juseyo
Please give me one ticket to 이태원 station.

직원: 900원입니다.
gubaek wonimnida
It is 900 won.

존 : 어느 쪽으로 가요?
eoneu jjogeuro gayo
Which way do I go?

직원: 저 표시를 따라가세요.
jeo pyosireul ttaragaseyo
Please follow the sign over there.

존 : 감사합니다. Thank you.
gamsahamnida

(지하철을 탄다.) Take the subway.
jihacheoreul tanda

지하철 방송: 다음 역은 이태원역입니다.
daeum yeogeun itaewon-yeogimnida
The next station is 이태원.

내리실 문은 왼쪽입니다.
naerisil muneun oenjjogimnida
The exit is on the left.

Vocabulary and Phrases

• 900원	900 won
• 어떻게	how
• 지하철	subway
• 6호선	line 6
• 이태원 역	Itaewon station
• 내리세요	to get off
• 타세요	to get on
• 왼쪽	left side
• 어떻게 가요?	How do I get to ...?
• 걸려요	to take(referring to time)
• 내리실 문	exit (the door that you get off)
• 어느	which
• 어느 쪽	which way
• 저기	over there
• 표시	sign
• 따라가세요	to follow
• 다음	next
• 다음 역	next station
• 걸어서	on foot

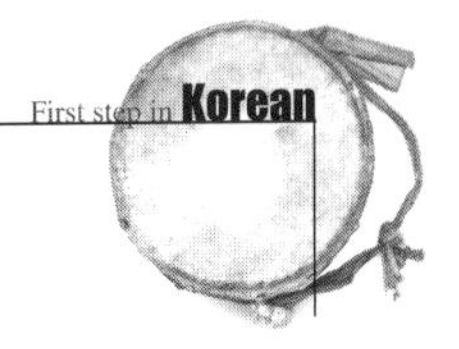

Word Drills

Means of transportation

자전거 bicycle
jajeongeo

오토바이 motorcycle
otobai

승용차 car
seungyongcha

버스 bus
beos

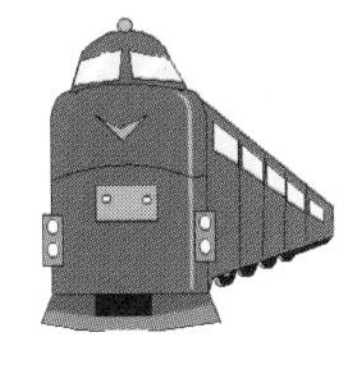

기차 train
gicha

지하철 subway
jihacheol

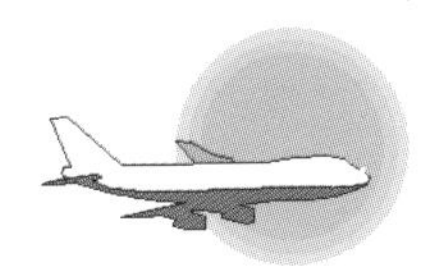

비행기 airplane
bihaenggi

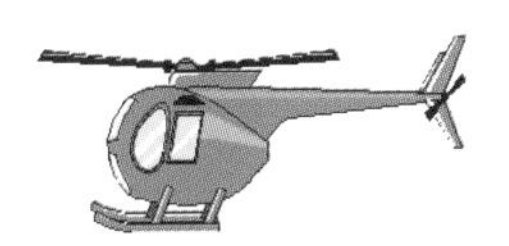

헬리콥터 helicopter
hellikopteo

여객선 passenger ship
yeogaekseon

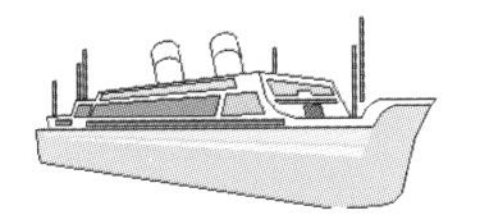

유람선 cruise ship
yuramseon

트럭 truck
teureok

택시 taxi
taeksi

Structures and Expressions

1 When you want to know how to get to a place, use the following expression.

__________ 은(는) 어떻게 가요? : How do I get to __________ ?

맥도날드
maekdonaldeu
McDonald's

지하철 역
jihacheolyeok
subway station

이태원
itaewon
Itaewon

학교
hakgyo
school

출입국 관리 사무소
churipguk gwanri samuso
immigration office

② When you want to get directions, use the following expression.

_________ **으로 가요?** : Which way do I go?

어느 쪽 which way
eoneu jjok

이쪽 this way
ijjok

저쪽 that way
jeojjok

그쪽 that way
geujjok

③ When you suggest the means of transportation, use the following expression.

_________ **(을)를 타세요.** : Take __________ .

지하철 subway
jihacheol

택시 taxi
taeksi

승용차 car
seungyongcha

버스 bus
beos

자전거 bicycle
jajeongeo

오토바이 motorcycle
otobai

Exercices

1 Complete the following sentences using the words in the boxes. (1)~(3)

(1)

Example
이태원, 김포공항, 여의도, 한강시민공원, 롯데월드, 민속촌

① ______________ 은(는) 어떻게 가요?

② ______________ 은(는) 어떻게 가요?

③ ______________ 은(는) 어떻게 가요?

④ ______________ 은(는) 어떻게 가요?

⑤ ______________ 은(는) 어떻게 가요?

(2)

Example
기차, 배, 버스, 택시, 승용차

① ______________ 을(를) 타고 가(세)요.

② ______________ 을(를) 타고 가(세)요.

③ ______________ 을(를) 타고 가(세)요.

④ ______________ 을(를) 타고 가(세)요.

⑤ ______________ 을(를) 타고 가(세)요.

(3)

Example
지하철을(를) 타세요.

① ______________ (버스 bus)

② ______________ (택시 taxi)

③ ______________ (유람선 cruise ship)

④ ______________ (오토바이 motorcycle)

⑤ ______________ (자전거 bicycle)

2 Provide an answer for the question in the box, using the direction words in parenthesis.

Example
어느 쪽으로 가야 돼요?

(1) ______________ 으로 가세요. (왼쪽 left side)

(2) ______________ 으로 가세요. (오른쪽 right side)

(3) ______________ 으로 가세요. (이쪽 this way)

(4) ______________ 으로 가세요. (저쪽 that way)

(5) ______________ 가세요. (곧장 straight)

3 Complete the following sentences, using the names of places that you know.

(1) ______________________ 에 가요.

(2) ______________________ 에 가요.

(3) ______________________ 에 가요.

(4) ______________________ 에 가요.

(5) ______________________ 에 가요.

Reading Practice

(1) 소라 씨, 집에는 어떻게 가요?
Sora, how do you get to your house?

(2) 서울역 한 장 주세요.
Please give me one ticket to Seoul station.

(3) 어느 쪽으로 가세요?
Which way are you going?

(4) 지하철로 얼마나 걸려요?
How long does it take by subway?

(5) 어디에서 내리세요?
Where do you get off?

제 12 과
Lesson 12

저는 내일 여행 갈 거예요.
I'm Going on a Trip Tomorrow.

Key Sentences

1. 저는 내일 여행 갈 거예요. I am going to go on a trip tomorrow.
   jeoneun naeil yeohaeng gal geoyeyo
2. 무궁화호 한 장 주세요. Please give me a ticket for the Mugungwha.
   mugunghwaho han jang juseyo

Dialogs

Dialog 1

존 : 저는 내일 여행 갈 거예요.
jeoneun naeil yeohaeng gal geoyeyo
I'm going to go on a trip tomorrow.

유미: 어디 가세요?
eodi gaseyo
Where are you going?

존 : 경주에 갈 거예요. I'm going to Gyeongju.
gyeongjue gal geoyeyo

한국의 전통적인 도시를 보고 싶어요.
hangugui jeontongjeogin dosireul bogo sipeoyo
I want to see some traditional cities in Korea.

유미: 불국사가 가장 유명해요. 꼭 가 보세요.
bulguksaga gajang yumyeonghaeyo kkok ga boseyo
Bulguksa (the Buddhist temple) is the most famous.
You must go.

좋은 여행 되세요. Have a nice trip.
joeun yeohaeng doeseyo

Dialog 2

존 : 3시 30분 무궁화호 한 장 주세요.
sesi samsipbun mugunghwaho han jang juseyo
Please give me one 3:30 Mugunghwa ticket.

직원 : 어디 가세요? Where are you going?
eodi gaseyo

존 : 설악산에 갑니다.
seoraksane gamnida
I'm going to Seorak mountain.

직원 : 조금 늦으셨어요. 방금 떠났어요.
jogeum neujeusyeosseoyo bang-geum tteonasseoyo
You are a little late. It has just left.

존 : 다음 열차는 몇 시에 있습니까?
daum yeolchaneun myeot sie itseumnikka
When is the next train?

직원 : 4시 10분 새마을호입니다.
nesi sipbun saemaeulhoimnida
It's the Saemaul at 4:10.

존 : 새마을호 한 장 주세요.
saemaeulho han jang juseyo
Please give me one ticket for the Saemaeul.

Vocabulary and Phrases

- 내일 tomorrow
- 여행 trip
- 갈 거예요 will go
- 어디 where
- 가세요? Do (you) go ...?
- 표 ticket
- 갑니다 to go
- 전통적인 traditional
- 보고 싶어요 want to see
- 몇 시? What time?
- 주세요 Please give me ...
- 보다 to see
- 가장 the most/best
- 유명한 famous
- 가 보세요 to go and see
- 꼭 surely
- 좋은 good
- 도시 city
- 조금 a little/few
- 무궁화호 the Mugunghwa
- 새마을호 the Saemaeul
- 방금 just now
- 떠났어요 left
- 다음 next
- 열차 train
- 경주 Gyeongju
- 한국 Korea
- 늦다 to be late

Word Drills

Main train stations in Korea

서울역, 수원역, 대전역, 대구역, 동대구역, 부산역

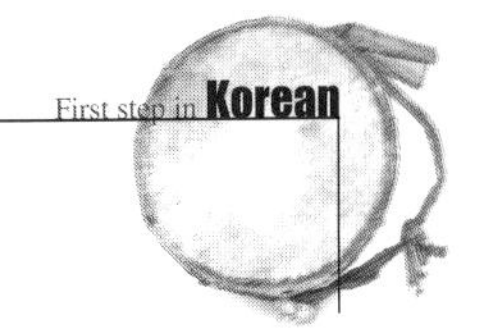

Types of trains

KTX(한국고속철도), 새마을호, 무궁화호

Counting tickets : number + 장 (numeral classifier)

네 장, 다섯 장, 여덟 장, 열 장, 열두 장

Main cities in Korea

서울, 부산, 인천, 대구, 광주, 대전, 울산, 제주, 춘천

Cities around Seoul

수원, 안양, 부천, 분당, 성남, 구리, 일산, 안산, 과천

Structures and Expressions

1. '가세요?' is analyzed as '가(다)+시+어요'. '시' is the honorific marker, and '어요' is the polite informal sentence ending. '시+어' is contracted to '셔' or '세' producing '가셔요?' or '가세요?' Note that '가세요/가셔요' can be the polite command ending with a falling intonation as in '안녕히 가세요/가셔요'.

어디 가세요? : Where are you going?

경주에 가세요?
gyeongjue gaseyo
Are you going to Gyeongju?

설악산에 가세요?
seoraksane gaseyo
Are you going to Seoraksan?

2. The postposition '~에' is used to indicate a direction in addition to a place or a time. '~에' can be replaced with '~로' to mean a direction.

경주에 갈 거예요.
gyeongjue gal geoyeyo
I will go to Gyeongju.

경주로 갈 거예요.
gyeongjuro gal geoyeyo
I will go to Gyeongju.

③ '~고 싶어요', is analyzed as 'verb stem + 고 + 싶(다) + 어요', meaning a wish, desire, or longing. The construction is used with the first person subject 'I' or 'we', which is usually deleted in Korean.

보고 싶어요 : want to see

경주를 보고 싶어요.
gyeongjureul bogo sipeoyo
I want to see Gyeoungju.

수미를 보고 싶어요.
sumireul bogo sipeoyo
I want to see Sumi.

④ '가장' makes the superlative constructions to express 'most', while '더' makes the comparative constructions to express 'more'.

가장 유명해요 : to be the most famous

불국사가 가장 유명해요.
bulguksaga gajang yumyeonghaeyo
Bulguksa is the most famous.

불국사가 해인사보다 더 유명해요.
bulguksaga haeinsaboda deo yumyeonghaeyo
Bulguksa is more famous than Haeinsa.

⑤ The expression '좋은 ~이(가) 되세요' is a kind of farewell greeting, meaning 'Have a nice ~'.

좋은 여행 되세요. : Have a nice trip.

좋은 밤 되세요.
joeun bam doeseyo
Have a nice night.

좋은 주말 되세요.
joeun jumal doeseyo
Have a good weekend.

⑥ To get train tickets, tell the ticket person the departure time, type of trains, and number of tickets. When you count tickets, use the numeral classifier '장' after the number. The appropriate verb to order tickets is '주세요 (give)'.

Time	Type of train	Number of tickets
3시 30분	무궁화호 Mugunghwaho	한 장 han jang
4시	KTX	두 장 du jang
5시	새마을호 Saemaeulho	세 장 se jang

Exercises

1 Using each word in parenthesis, provide an answer for the question in the box.

> **Example**
> Question : 어디 가십니까?

(1) Answer : ______________ 갑니다. (강릉)

(2) Answer : ______________ 갑니다. (경주)

(3) Answer : ______________ 갑니다. (설악산)

(4) Answer : ______________ 갑니다. (지리산)

(5) Answer : ______________ 갑니다. (남해안)

2 Provide an appropriate verb form to express the meaning in parenthesis.

(1) 판교로 ______________ . (go)

(2) 안양에 ______________ . (will go)

(3) 용인에 ______________ . (will go)

(4) 광주로 ______________ . (want to go)

(5) 분당으로 ______________ . (go)

3 Complete the following sentences using the information in parenthesis.

(1) 표 ________ 주세요. (5 tickets)

(2) 표 ________ 주세요. (10 tickets)

(3) 표 ________ 주세요. (7 tickets)

(4) 표 ________ 주세요. (11 tickets)

(5) 표 ________ 주세요. (14 tickets)

4 Complete the sentences using the example in the box.

> **Example**
> 두 시 무궁화호 한 장 주세요.

(1) ______________________________ 주세요.

(2) ______________________________ 주세요.

(3) ______________________________ 주세요.

(4) ______________________________ 주세요.

(5) ______________________________ 주세요.

5 Complete the sentences below to order tickets.

(1) 새마을호 ______________________________ .

(2) KTX ______________________________ .

(3) 고속버스 ______________________________ .

(4) 무궁화호 침대칸 ______________________ .

Reading Practice

(1) 저는 모레 여행을 떠날 거예요.
I'm going on a trip the day after tomorrow.

(2) 설악산을 보고 싶어요.
I want to see Seoraksan.

(3) 경주에 가고 싶어요.
I want to go to Gyeongju.

(4) 불국사가 가장 유명해요.
Bulguksa is the most famous.

(5) 새마을호 한 장 주세요.
Please give me one Saemaeulho ticket.

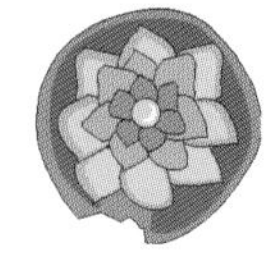

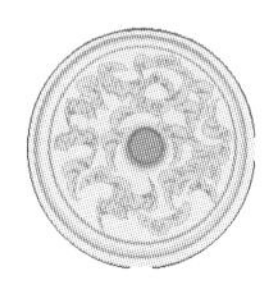

제 13 과

Lesson 13

방 구하기 Renting a House

Key Sentences

1. 자취방 있어요? Do you have a room for rent?
   jachwibang isseoyo
2. 계약서를 작성합시다. Let's fill out the contract.
   gyeyakseoreul jakseonghapsida

Dialogs

Dialog 1

존 : 자취방 있어요?
jachwibang isseoyo
Is there a self-boarding room?

주인: 이쪽으로 앉으세요. Please have a seat over here.
ijjogeuro anjeuseyo

존 : 얼마 정도 합니까?
eolma jeongdo hamnikka
About how much is it?

주인: 보증금 100만 원에 월 10만 원 정도예요.
bojeung-geum baekman wone wol sipman won jeongdoyeyo
It's about 1 million won for the deposit and 100,000 won monthly rent.

존 : 집 구경할 수 있어요?
jip gugyeonghal su isseoyo
Can I take a look at the house?

주인: 예, 지금 같이 가 보시겠습니까?
ye jigeum gachi ga bosigetseumnikka
Yes, would you like to have a look now?

Dialog 2

주인: 이 방입니다. This is the room.
i bang-imnida

존 : 방이 깨끗하고 좋군요. It's great and clean.
bang-i kkaekkeutago jokunyo

이 방으로 하겠습니다.
i bang-euro hagetseumnida
I would like to take this room.

주인: 사무실에서 계약서를 작성하도록 합시다.
samusileseo gyeyakseoreul jakseonghadorok hapsida
Let's fill out the contract at the office.

주인: 여기에 이름과 주소와 여권 번호를 적어 주세요.
yeogie ireumgwa jusowa yeogwon beonhoreul jeogeo juseyo
Please fill out your name, address, and passport number here.

그리고 계약 기간은 1년으로 하시겠어요?
geurigo gyeyak giganeun ilnyeoneuro hasigesseoyo
And would you like the term of the contract to be a year?

존 : 예, 1년으로 하겠습니다.
ye ilnyeoneuro hagtseumnida
Yes, I would like to make it one year.

주인: 계약금을 지불하시겠어요?
Gyeyaggeumeul jibulhasigesseoyo
Would you make a down payment?

존 : 예, 여기 있습니다.
ye yeogi itseumnida
Yes, here it is.

(표준계약서식) **부동산임대차계약서** (월세)

임대인과 임차인은 아래 표시 부동산에 관하여 다음 계약내용과 같이 합의하여 임대차 계약을 체결한다.

1. 부동산의 표시

소재지				
토지	지목		면적	㎡(평)
건물	구조·용도		면적	㎡(평)
임대할부분				

2. 계약내용

제1조: 위 부동산의 임대차에 있어 임차인은 임대차 보증금 및 차임을 아래와 같이 지불하기로 한다.

보증금	금 원정 (₩)
계약금	금 원정은 계약시 지불하고
중도금	금 원정은 19 년 월 일 지불하며
잔금	금 원정은 19 년 월 일 중개업자 입회하에 지불한다.
차임	금 원정을 매월 일까지 지급하기로 한다.

제2조: 임대차 기간은 19 년 월 일부터 19 년 월 일까지로 한다.
제3조: 임대인은 위 부동산을 임대차 목적대로 사용·수익할 수 있는 상태로 하여 19 년 월 일까지 임차인에게 인도한다.
제4조: 임차인은 임대인의 동의 없이는 위 부동산의 용도나 구조 등을 변경하거나 전대·임차권 양도 또는 담보제공을 하지 못하며 차임을 2회이상 지불하지 않은 경우, 임대인은 최고없이 이 계약을 해지하고 위 부동산의 반환을 요구할 수 있다.
제5조: 임차인이 임대인에게 중도금(중도금약정이 없을 때에는 잔금)을 지불하기 전까지는 임대인은 계약금의 배액으로 상환하고, 임차인 또한 계약금을 포기하고 이 계약을 해제할 수 있다.
제6조: 임대차물건에 관한 중개수수료는 이 계약 체결과 동시에 계약 당사자 쌍방이 각각 지불한다.
※ 특약사항 :

이 계약을 증명하기 위하여 계약당사자가 이의 없음을 확인하고 각자 서명·날인한다.

3. 계약당사자 및 중개업자 19 년 월 일

임대인	주소					
	주민등록번호		전화		성명	인
임차인	주소					
	주민등록번호		전화		성명	인
중개업자	사무소소재지					
	사무소명칭					
	대표		인			인
	허가번호		전화		전화	
	사업자등록번호					

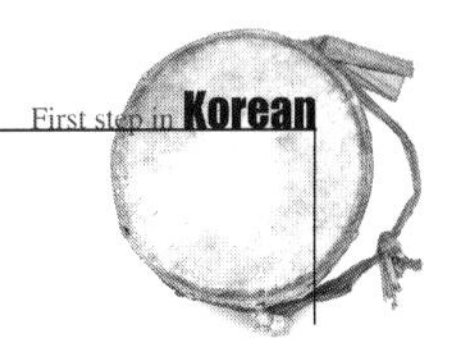

Vocabulary and Phrases

- 부동산 real estate
- 월 monthly
- 좋다 good
- 돈 money
- 깨끗하다 to be clean
- 작성하다 to fill out
- 계약금 down payment
- 집 구경 look around the house
- 앉다 to seat
- 지금 now
- 계약서 contract
- 얼마 정도 about how much
- 사무실 office
- 정도 approximately, about
- 자취방 a self-boarding room
- 계약 기간 terms of a contract
- 보증금 deposit
- 방 room
- 합시다 let's
- 같이 together, with
- 1년으로 by a year
- 할 수 있어요? can I?

Word Drills

Types of apartment renting in Korea

전세 jeonse rent a house with key money
월세 wolse monthly rent
자취 jachwi self-boarding room
하숙 hasuk boarding house

Structures and Expressions

1. When you ask about approximate price, size, and duration, use the expression '얼마 정도 합니까?/됩니까?/입니까?' respectively. The expression is analyzed as '얼마(how much)+정도(about, degree, approximately)+합니까?/됩니까?/입니까?(to be)'.

얼마 정도 합니까? / 얼마 정도 됩니까? / 얼마 정도입니까?
: About how much is it?

이 아파트는 얼마 정도 합니까?
i apateuneun eolma jeongdo hamnikka
About how much is this apartment?

방 크기는 얼마 정도 됩니까?
bang keugineun eolma jeongdo doemnikka
About how big is the room?

계약 기간은 얼마 정도입니까?
gyeyak giganeun eolma jeongdoimnikka
About how long is the term of the contract?

② The expression '~(으)ㄹ 수 있다' corresponds to the English modal auxiliary 'can'. To make the polite informal style question, attach '~어요?' after the verb stem '~있'.

아파트를 구경할 수 있어요? : Can I take a look at the apartment?

오늘 만날 수 있어요?
oneul mannal su isseoyo
Can I see you today?

김치를 먹을 수 있어요?
kimchireul meogeul su isseoyo
Can you eat kimchi?

③ The future tense marker '~겠' is used to indicate the future tense. It is used for both a statement and a question.

이 방으로 하겠습니다. : I will take this room.

내일 다시 오겠습니다.
naeil dasi ogetseumnida
I will come back tomorrow.

내일 거기 가겠습니다.
naeil geogi gagetseumnida
I will go there tomorrow.

영화관에 같이 가시겠습니까?
yeonghwagwane gachi gasigetseumnikka
Will you go to the movie theater with (me)?

④ The expression '~고' coordinates two adjectives, which means 'and'.

깨끗하고 좋다. : clean and good

하늘이 파랗고 맑다.
haneuri parako makda
The sky is blue and clear.

음식이 짜고 맵다.
eumsigi jjago maepda
This dish is salty and spicy.

⑤ The expression '~과/와' is used to coordinate nouns. '~과' is used after a noun that ends with a consonant, while '~와' is used after a noun that ends with a vowel.

이름과 주소와 여권 번호 : name, address and passport number

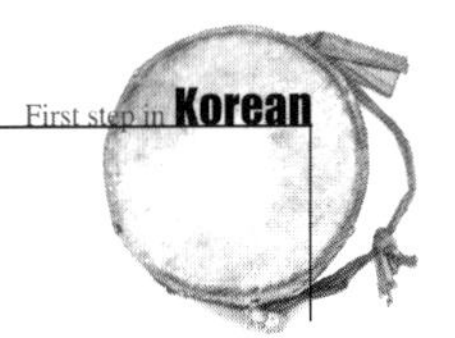

바나나와 사과와 오렌지 bananas, apples and oranges
bananawa sagwawa orenji

음식과 음료수 food and drinks
eumsikgwa eumryosu

⑥ The construction '~하도록/하기로 합시다' is used to suggest an idea, meaning 'Let's ...'. Due to the honorific marker '~시' and the sentence ending '다', it makes the polite formal style. The non polite informal counterpart is '~하도록/하기로 하자'.

계약서를 작성하도록 합시다. : Let's fill out the contract form.

공부를 하도록 합시다. Let's study.
gongbureul hadorok hapsida

불고기를 먹도록 합시다.
bulgogireul meokdorok hapsida
Let's eat Bulgogi.

공부를 하도록 하자. Let's study.
gongbureul hadorok haja

불고기를 먹도록 하자.
bulgogireul meokdorok haja
Let's eat Bulgogi.

Exercises

1 Change the verb form following the examples in the box.

Example
하다 → 할 수 있다 can do
먹다 → 먹을 수 있다 can eat

(1) 쓰다 → _______ can write (2) 가져오다 → _____ can bring

(3) 가다 → _______ can go (4) 사다 → _____ can buy

2 Practice counting money as shown in the example.

Example
1,000,000원 → 백만 원

(1) 2,500,000원 → __________ (2) 3,000,000원 → __________

(3) 450,000원 → __________ (4) 150,000,000원 → __________

3 Change the verb form as shown in the example.

Exemple

가다 → 가겠어요 → 가겠습니다 → 가시겠어요?

(1) 오다 to come → ________ → ________ → ________ ?

(2) 잡다 to grab → ________ → ________ → ________ ?

(3) 놀다 to play → ________ → ________ → ________ ?

(4) 믿다 to believe → ________ → ________ → ________ ?

(5) 하다 to do → ________ → ________ → ________ ?

4 Coordinate the following nouns with an appropriate conjunct.

(1) 이름, 주소, 여권 번호

(2) 가방, 열쇠, 수첩

(3) 컴퓨터, 디스켓, 프린트

(4) 갈비, 설렁탕, 냉면

(5) 한국 사람, 나이지리아 사람, 케냐 사람

5 Coordinate the following adjectives with an appropriate conjunct.

(1) 아름답다(beautiful), 깨끗하다(clean)

(2) 고요하다(quiet), 아늑하다(snug), 넓다(spacious)

(3) 착하다(honest), 정직하다(righteous)

Reading Practice

(1) 자취방 있어요? Do you have a self-boarding room?

(2) 계약을 하시겠어요? Would you like to sign the contract?

(3) 계약 기간은 1년입니다. The term of the contract is for one year.

(4) 사무실에서 계약서를 작성합시다.
Let's fill out the contract at the office.

(5) 지금 방 구경을 할 수 있을까요?
Would it be possible to have a look at the room now?

제 14 과
Lesson 14

은행에서 At the Bank

Key Sentences

1. 통장을 만들려고 하는데요. I'd like to open a bank account.
   tongjang-eul mandeulryeogo haneundeyo
2. 돈을 찾으려고 하는데요. I'd like to withdraw some money.
   doneul chajeuryeogo haneundeyo

Dialogs

Dialog 1

존 : 통장을 만들려고 하는데요.
tongjang-eul mandeulryeogo haneundeyo
I'd like to open a bank account.

은행원: 신청서를 작성해 주세요.
sincheongseoreul jakseonghae juseyo
Please fill out the application form.

존 : 여기에는 무엇을 씁니까?
yeogieneun mueoseul sseumnikka
What do I write here?

은행원: 여권 번호를 써 주세요.
yeogwon beonhoreul sseo juseyo
Please write down your passport number.

그리고 도장과 신분증을 주세요.
geurigo dojang-gwa sinbunjeung-eul juseyo
And please give me your signature stamp and a piece of identification.

존 : 다 썼는데 이제 어떻게 하지요?
da sseonneunde ije eotteoke hajiyo
I've filled it all out, and what should I do now?

은행원: 잠시만 기다려 주세요. Please wait a minute.
jamsiman gidaryeo juseyo

(잠시 후)(In a while)

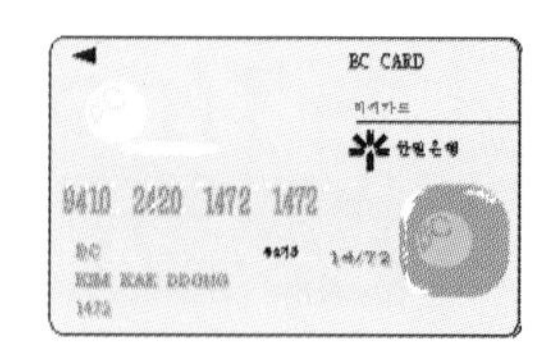

은행원: 여기 통장과 현금 카드가 있습니다.
yeogi tongjanggwa hyeongeum kadeuga itseumnida
Here's your bankbook and cash card.

존 : 감사합니다. gamsahamnida Thank you.

Dialog 2

존 : 돈을 찾으려고 하는데요. I'd like to make a withdrawal.
doneul chajeuryeogo haneundeyo

은행원: 통장과 지급 신청서를 작성해 주세요.
tongjang-gwa jigeub sincheongseoreul jakseonghae juseyo
Please give me your bankbook and the withdrawal slip.

도장을 주시고, 비밀 번호를 적어 주세요.
dojang-eul jusigo bimil beonhoreul jeogeo juseyo
Please give me your signature stamp, and write down your Personal Identification Number (PIN).

존 : 여기 있습니다. yeogi itseumnida Here they are.

은행원: 여기 십만 원짜리 수표 한 장과 현금 3만 원입니다.
yeogi sipman won jjari supyo han janggwa hyeongeum samman wonimnida
Here is a 100,000 won check and 30,000 won in cash.

확인해 보세요.
hwaginhae boseyo
Please check it.

존 : 감사합니다.
gamsahamnida
Thank you.

찾으실 때		입금하실 때	
금 원 (₩)		계좌번호	- -
		성 명	☎

계 좌 번 호			
대 체			
현 금			
지급회차지정시		수수료	
위와 같이 지급하여 주십시오. (이 예금/신탁의 최종계산을 승인합니다.) 예금주 (인) (수익자) (서명)		실명확인	절차확인
		인 감 대 조	
비 밀 번 호			

금 액			
대 체			
현 금			
타점권			
수표발행	1매당 발행금액	매수	금 액
	10만원권		
	만원권		
합 계			

입 금 요구서	계좌번호	
	성 명	
	금 액	

수수료 ______

평생은행

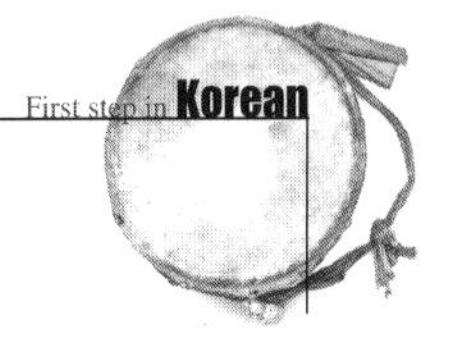

Vocabulary and Phrases

- 통장 bankbook
- 기다리다 to wait
- 수표 check
- 저금하다 to deposit
- 쓰다 to write
- 현금 카드 cash card
- 확인하다 to check
- 확인하다 to confirm
- 지급 신청서 withdrawal slip
- 비밀 번호 Personal Identification Number (PIN)
- 여권 번호 passport number
- 만들다 to make
- 돈 money
- 적다 to write down
- 만들려고 to make
- 그리고 and
- 찾다(인출하다) to withdraw
- 확인해 보다 try to check
- 신청서 application form
- 도장 stamp used as a signature
- 모두 all
- 인출 withdrawal
- 현금 cash
- 작성하다 to fill out
- 신분증 ID card

Structures and Expressions

① The connective '~(으)려고' expresses an intention of the subject, preceded by the verb '~하다 (do)'. The connective ending '~(는)데요', produces a connective meaning such as 'and', 'but' or 'by the way'. This ending is used to open a question or a request or to solicit a response for the question in mind.

통장을 만들려고 하는데요. : I would like to open an account.

한국어를 배우려고 하는데요.
hangugeoreul baeuryeogo haneundeyo
I would like to study the Korean language.

도서관에서 책을 읽으려고 하는데요.
doseogwaneseo chaegeul ilgeuryeogo haneundeyo
I would like to read a book at the library.

② '~아/어 주세요', can be used as a main verb or an auxiliary verb. When it is used as a main verb, it means 'give'. On the other hand, when it is used as an auxiliary verb, it supports the main verb, meaning 'Please do it for me'.

써 주세요. : Please write (it down for me).

여권 번호를 써 주세요.
yeogwon beonhoreul sseo juseyo
Please write down the passport number (for me).

신청서를 작성해 주세요.
sincheongseoreul jakseonghae juseyo
Please fill out the application form (for me).

비밀 번호를 적어 주세요.
bimil beonhoreul jeogeo juseyo
Please write down the PIN number (for me).

잠시만 기다려 주세요. Please wait a minute (for me).
jamsiman gidaryeo juseyo

③ The topic marker '~는' can be used not only for the subject but for postpositional phrases.

여기에는 무엇을 씁니까? : What do I write in here?

④ '~고' coordinates two clauses, expressing a simple coordination of events or a sequential ordering of events.

도장을 주시고 비밀 번호를 적어 주세요. : Please give me the signature stamp and write down the PIN.

신청서를 작성하고 사인해 주세요.
sincheongseoreul jakseonghago sainhae juseyo
Fill out an application form and sign it please.

통장은 여기 있고 현금 카드는 여기 있습니다.
tongjang-eun yeogi itgo hyeon-geumkadeuneun yeogi itseumnida
Here is the bankbook and here is the cash card.

⑤ '~아/어 보세요' is used as an auxillary verb to support the main verb. When it is used as a main verb, it expresses the meaning 'see', but when it is used as an auxilliary verb, it means 'try to do'.

확인해 보세요. : Try to check (it).

찾아보세요. Try to look for (something).
chajaboseyo

가 보세요. Try to go (there).
ga boseyo

기다려 보세요. Try to wait.
gidaryeo boseyo

1 Complete the following dialogs, following the examples. (1)~(3)

(1)

Example
여기에는 무엇을 씁니까? (여권 번호 passport number) → 여권 번호를 써 주세요.
What do I write in here? → Please write down your passport number.

① 여기에는 무엇을 씁니까? (생년월일 birth date)
→ ____________________

② 여기에는 무엇을 씁니까? (이름 name)
→ ____________________

③ 여기에는 무엇을 씁니까? (비밀 번호 Personal Identification Number)
→ ____________________

④ 여기에는 무엇을 씁니까? (현주소 present address)
→ ____________________

(2)

Example
통장을 만들다 → 통장을 만들려고 하는데요.
to open a bank account → I would like to open a bank account.

① 집에 가다 to go home
→ ____________________

② 공원에서 놀다 to play in the park
→ ____________________

③ 오늘 식당에서 밥을 먹다 to eat in a restaurant today
→ ____________________

④ 도서관에서 공부를 하다 to study in the library
→ ____________________

⑤ 방에서 책을 읽다 to read books in the room
→ ____________________

(3)

Exemple

신청서를 작성하다 → 신청서를 작성해 주세요.
to fill out the application form   Please fill out the application form (for me).

① 여기에 쓰다 to write in here
→ ______________

② 학교에 가다 to go to school
→ ______________

③ 공책을 찾다 to find the notebook
→ ______________

④ 책을 읽다 to read books
→ ______________

⑤ 창문을 열다 to open the window
→ ______________

2 Combine the following clauses and make them into one sentence.

(1) 도장을 주세요. 비밀 번호를 적어 주세요.

(2) 수미는 학교에 갑니다. 헨리는 은행에 갑니다.

(3) 수미는 오렌지를 먹습니다. 헨리는 귤을 먹습니다.

3 Write the Korean sentence for 'Please wait a minute'.

Reading Practice

(1) 돈을 찾으려고 하는데요.
I'd like to withdraw some money.

(2) 지급 청구서를 작성해 주세요.
Please fill out a withdrawal slip.

(3) 비밀 번호, 도장, 주소, 여권이 필요합니다.
I'd need your PIN, signature stamp, address, and passport.

(4) 수표와 현금을 확인해 보세요.
Please verify the check and cash.

(5) 신분증을 주세요.
Please provide your identification.

제 15 과 Lesson 15

백화점에서 At the Department Store

Key Sentences

1. 운동화를 사려고 해요. I'd like to buy some sneakers.
   undonghwareul saryeogo haeyo
2. 사이즈는 어떻게 되요? What is your size?
   saijeuneun eotteoke doeyo

Dialogs

Dialog 1

안내원: 무슨 매장을 찾으십니까?
museun maejang-eul chajeusimnikka
What section are you looking for?

존 : 운동화를 사려고 해요.
undonghwareul saryeogo haeyo
I'd like to buy some sneakers.

안내원: 운동화는 6층에 있습니다.
undonghwaneun yukcheung-e itseumnida
Sneakers are on the 6th floor.

존 : 엘리베이터는 어디 있습니까? Where is the elevator?
ellibeiteoneun eodi itseumnikka

안내원: 엘리베이터는 저기에 있고, 에스컬레이터는 이쪽에 있습니다.
ellibeiteoneun jeogie itgo eskeolleiteoneun ijjoge itseumnida
The elevator is over there and the escalator is over here.

존 : 알겠습니다. I see.
algetseumnida

Dialog 2

존 : 운동화를 사려고 해요.
undonghwareul saryeogo haeyo
I'd like to buy some sneakers.

점원: 색깔은 파란색, 검은색, 흰색이 있어요.
saekkkareun paransaek geomeunsaek huinsaegi isseoyo
The colors are blue, black, and white.

상표는 나이키, 프로스펙스, 아디다스가 있어요.
sangpyoneun naiki peurospekseu adidaseuga isseoyo
The brands are Nike, Prospecs, and Addidas.

일반 상표도 저쪽에 있어요.
ilbansangpyodo jeojjoge isseoyo
The generic brands are over there.

존 : 흰색 나이키가 마음에 들어요.
huinsaek naikiga maeume deureoyo
I like the white Nikes.

그러나 일반 상표도 싸고 좋군요.
geureona ilbansangpyodo ssago jokunyo
But the generic brands are also inexpensive and good.

점원: 발 사이즈가 얼마입니까?
bal saijeuga eolmaimnikka
What is your foot size?

존 : 265mm예요. It's 265mm.
ibaek-yuksibo mirimiteoyeyo

점원: 한번 신어 보세요.
hanbeon sineo boseyo
Please try them on.

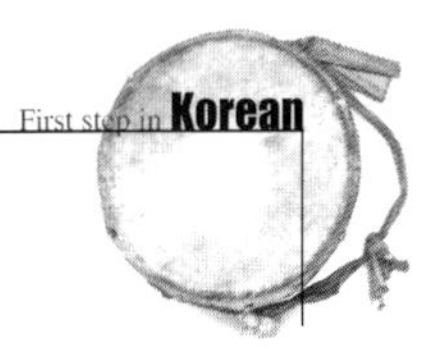

Vocabulary and Phrases

- 찾다 to search
- 엘리베이터 elevator
- 에스컬레이터 escalator
- 일반상표 generic brand
- 저기에 over there
- 검은색 black
- 백화점 department store
- 안내원 information personnel
- 운동화 sneakers
- 파란색 blue
- 흰색 white
- 마음에 in mind
- 발 foot
- 상표 brand
- 신다 to wear (for footwear)
- 사려고 해요 would like to buy
- 사이즈 size
- ~도 also
- 한번 once
- 사다 to buy
- 6층 6th floor
- 색깔 color

Word Drills

(For names of colors please refer to the page 6.)

Structures and Expressions

1. The connective '~(으)려고' expresses an intention of the subject, preceded by the verb '~하다' preceded by a noun, meaning 'what' in English.

운동화를 사려고 해요. : I would like to buy some sneakers.

운동화를 사려고 해요. undonghwareul saryeogo haeyo	I would like to buy some sneakers.
백화점에 가려고 해요. baekhwajeome garyeogo haeyo	I would like to go to the department store.

2. The verb '신어' derives from '신다'. '~어' is the connective which connects the verb to the following verb, producing '신어 보세요'. '보세요' is used as an auxiliary verb to support the main verb. When it is used as a main verb, it expresses the meaning 'see', but when it is used as an auxiliary verb, it means 'try to do'.

신어 보세요. : Try (it) on.

한번 입어 보세요.
hanbeon ibeo boseyo
Try (it) on once.

한번 먹어 보세요.
hanbeon meogeo boseyo
Taste (it) once.

③ Both the topic and the subject can coexist in a sentence as in '색깔은 흰색이 있어요'. And the subject can be made with conjoined nouns as in '파란색, 검은색, 흰색이 있어요'. Note that in Korean 'and' is optional for coordination of nouns: '파란색, 검은색, (그리고) 흰색이 있어요'.

색깔은 파란색, 검은색, 흰색이 있어요.
: As for colors, there is blue, black, and white.

동물은 호랑이, 원숭이, 곰이 있어요.
dongmureun horang-i wonsung-i gomi isseoyo
As for animals, there are tigers, monkeys, and bears.

신발은 운동화, 구두, 샌들이 있어요.
sinbareun undonghwa gudu saendeuri isseoyo
As for shoes, there are sneakers, dress shoes, and sandals.

④ '~도' replaces the subject or topic marker, meaning 'also' or 'too'.

일반 상표도 있어요. : We have generic brands too.

빨간색도 있어요.
ppalgansaekdo isseoyo
There is a red one, too.

연필도 있어요.
yeonpildo isseoyo
There is a pencil, too.

⑤ The polite sentence ending '~군요' expresses the speaker's new awareness of a fact or an event, '~고' coordinates two predicates '싸다' and '좋다'.

일반 상표도 싸고 좋군요. : Generic brands are also cheap and good.

나이키도 튼튼하고 좋군요.
naikido teunteunhago jokunyo
Nike is also durable and good.

흰색도 깨끗하고 예쁘군요.
huinsaekdo kkaekkeutago yeppeugunyo
White is also clean and pretty.

Exercises

1 Complete the dialogs following the example. (1)~(3)

(1)

Example
어느 매장을 찾으세요? (와이셔츠를 사다 buy a dress shirt)
Which section are you looking for?
→ 와이셔츠를 사려고 해요. I would like to buy a dress shirt.

① 어디를 찾으세요? (구두를 사다 buy dress shoes)
→ ______________________

② 어디를 찾으세요? (양복을 사다 buy a suit)
→ ______________________

③ 어디를 찾으세요? (색동이불을 사다 buy a colorful quilt)
→ ______________________

④ 어디를 찾으세요? (가전제품을 사다 buy home electric appliances)
→ ______________________

(2)

Example
식료품 매장은 어디입니까? (지하 1층 first floor basement)
Where is the food section?
→ 식료품 매장은 지하 1층입니다.
The food section is in the first floor basement.

① 의류 매장(apparel)은 어디입니까? (5층)
→ ______________________

② 신사복 매장(men's wear)은 어디입니까? (3층)
→ ______________________

③ 전자제품 매장(electronics)은 어디입니까? (7층)
→ ______________________

(3)

Example
얼마예요? (14,500원) How much is it?
→ 만 사천오백 원입니다. It is 14,500 won.

(1) 이 공책(notebook)은 얼마예요? (430원)
→ ______________________

(2) 이 주스(juice)는 얼마예요? (3,200원)
→ ______________________________

(3) 그 과자(snack)는 얼마예요? (2,800원)
→ ______________________________

2 Combine the following two sentences.

(1) 엘리베이터는 저기에 있습니다.
The elevator is over there.
에스컬레이터는 이쪽에 있습니다.
The escalator is over here.

(2) 운동화는 6층에 있어요.
Sneakers are on the 6th floor.
옷은 4층에 있어요.
Clothing is on the 4th floor.

(3) 프로스펙스는 이쪽에 있어요.
Prospecs is over here.
일반 상표는 저쪽에 있어요.
Generic brands are over there.

3 Change the following sentences using '～도'.

(1) 일반 상표가 싸고 좋아요. Generic brands are cheap and good.
→ ______________________________

(2) 검은색이 좋아요. Black is good.
→ ______________________________

(3) 사과가 좋아요. Apples are good.
→ ______________________________

(4) 바지가 좋아요. Pants are good.
→ ______________________________

(5) 한국어가 좋아요. The Korean language is good.
→ ______________________________

Reading Practice

(1) 셔츠를 사려고 해요. I'd like to buy a shirt.

(2) 운동화는 4층에 있어요. Sneakers are on the 4th floor.

(3) 목 사이즈가 얼마입니까? What is your neck size?

(4) 검정색 프로스펙스 운동화가 마음에 들어요.
I like the black Prospecs.

(5) 한번 신어 보세요. Please try them on.

제 16 과
Lesson 16
편지 쓰기 Writing a Letter

Key Sentences

1. 어떻게 지내셨습니까? — How have you been?
   eotteoke jinaesyeotseumnikka
2. 연락을 기다리겠습니다. — I will be waiting for your reply.
   yeollageul gidarigetseumnida

알 림
Notice

사무엘 로이그 씨에게 (Dear Mr. Samuel Roig,)
samuel roigeu ssiege

안녕하세요? 어떻게 지내셨습니까? 태평양 대학교 한국어반 졸업생과 재학생의 친목 모임이 있습니다. 부디 오셔서 동문들과 의미 있는 시간을 가지시기 바랍니다.
annyeonghaseyo eotteoke jinaesyeotseumnikka taepyeongyang daehakgyo hankugeoban joreopsaenggwa jaehaksaeng-ui chinmok moimi itseumnida budi osyeoseo dongmundeulgwa uimiinneun siganeul gajisigi baramnida
(Hello? How have you been? There is a get-together for graduates and undergraduates of the Taepyeongyang University Korean class. Please come and have an enjoyable time with us.)

일 시 : 5월 5일 (Date)
장 소 : 종로 2가 미리내 레스토랑 (Place)
시 간 : 12:00 PM (Time)
준비물 : 식사비 (Requirement : Lunch Money)

만나 뵙기를 바랍니다. 안녕히 계십시오.
manna boepgireul baramnida annyeonghi gyesipsio
(I look forward to seeing you at that time.)

2004년 4월 20일(April 20, 2004)
존 알렌 올림(John Allen)
한국어반 동문회장(Alumni president of the Korean class)

초 대 장
Invitation

유미 씨에게 (Dear Yumi,)
yumi ssiege

어떻게 지내셨어요?
이번 3월 17일에 존의 생일 파티가 있습니다. 하지만 존에게는 비밀이에요. 깜짝파티를 해 주고 싶거든요. 시간이 나면 저의 집으로 5시까지 오세요. 낸시와 가드윈 그리고 차오민도 올 것입니다. 존에게는 7시에 잠시 들르라고 부탁했어요.

eotteoke jinaesyeosseoyo
ibeon samwol sipchilile jonui saeng-il patiga itseumnida hajiman jonegeneun bimirieyo kkamjjak patireul haejugo sipgeodeunyo sigani namyeon jeoui jibeuro daseotsikkaji oseyo naensiwa gadeuwin geurigo chaomindo ol geosimnida jonegeneun ilgopsie jamsi deulreurago butakhaesseoyo

(How have you been?
There is a birthday party for John on March 17th, but it is a secret to John. We'd like it to be a surprise party. If you are available, please come to my house by 5 o'clock. Nancy, Godwin, and Chaomin will be coming. I've asked John to come by for a few minutes at 7 o'clock.)

회답을 기다릴게요. (I will be waiting for your reply.)
hoedabeul gidarilgeyo

안녕히 계세요. (Good bye.)
annyeonghi geseyo

2004년 3월 5일(Mar. 5, 2004)
브라이언 드림(Brian)

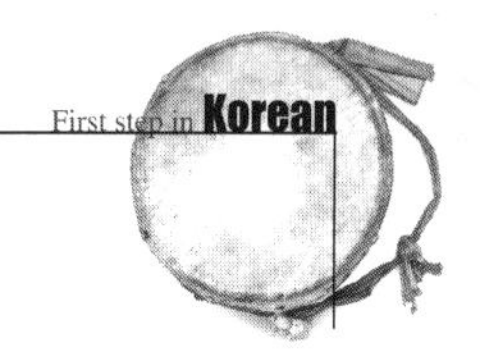

Vocabulary and Phrases

- 알림 notice
- 졸업생 graduate
- 가지다 to have, spend
- 깜짝파티 surprise party
- 오세요 please come
- 한국어반 Korean class
- 바라다 to hope
- 초대장 invitaion card
- 비밀 secret
- 올 것이다 will come
- ~고 싶다 want to
- 생일파티 birthday party
- 시간이 나다 to have time
- 모임 gathering/get together
- 그 동안 while
- 친목 making friends
- 준비물 preparation
- 잘 well
- 기다리다 to wait
- 재학생 enrolled students
- 장소 place
- 연락 reply
- 부탁하다 to ask
- 들르다 to come by/visit
- 잠시 for a few minutes
- 해 주다 to serve/give
- 동문회 alumni association
- 지내다 to live
- 부디 please
- 집 house
- 오다 to come
- ~씨에게 Dear~/To
- 이번 this time
- 그날 that day
- 하지만 but
- ~까지 to
- 의미있는 meaningful
- 동문 alumni

Word Drills

그저께	the day before yesterday
어제	yesterday
오늘	today

Structures and Expressions

1. Write the recipient's name and attach '~씨/~님에게' before you start the body of a letter. '~에게' can be replaced with its honorific counterpart '~께'. In case of children, attach only '~에게'.

사무엘 로이그 씨에게	Dear Samuel Roig
김유리 씨께	Dear Kim Yuri
이선미 선생님께	Dear teacher Lee Seonmi
지미에게	Dear Jimi (child)

② Start with greetings as shown in the box below.

> **안녕하세요? 어떻게 지내셨습니까?**
> : How are you? How have you been?

③ End with the following sentences as shown in the box below.

> **회답을 기다릴게요. 안녕히 계십시오. / 안녕히 계세요.**
> : I will wait for your reply. Good bye.
> **만나 뵙기를 바랍니다. 안녕히 계십시오.**
> : I will look forward to seeing you. Good bye.

④ Unlike the English letter form, you should write the date in the end with your signature. After the signature, you should attach '드림' or '올림'. '올림' is used, when you write to people who are higher in social status or older, and '드림' is used for more intimate and closer people. If you are writing to your friends or to people who are younger, these formalities are not needed, '씀' can be optionally used in this case.

2004년 1월 28일 존 알렌 올림	2004년 2월 3일 사무엘 로이그 드림	2004년 3월 2일 김유리 씀

서울특별시 은평구 대조동 1번지
태평양 대학교 한국어반
이영주 올림
122-837

stamp

경기도 안양시 만안구 박달 2동
사무엘 로이그 귀하
430-032

1 Before you use the greetings, what is needed in a letter form? Provide an answer using the following names.

(1) 이수미 → ________

(2) 존 알렌 → ________

(3) 김유리 → ________

(4) 이영주 선생님 → ________

(5) 박지미(child) → ________

2 Provide greetings to start a letter.

→ ____

3 Provide farewell greetings to end a letter.

→ ____

4 Write the date and signature in accordance with the letter formality, using the following dates and names.

(1) 2004년 1월 5일, 김영자 (She is writing to her parents.)

(2) 2004년 2월 21일, 이인수 (He is writing to his teacher.)

(3) 2004년 3월 13일, 박혜진 (She is writing to her friends.)

5 Write a letter to inform the students in a Korean class of a picnic at Everland. They are supposed to meet at 11 : 00 AM at the gate on May 5. Follow the letter format carefully.

6 Write an informal letter to your Korean friend.

7 Using addresses of the sender and the recipient, fill in the envelope according to the proper letter format. The recipient's social status is higher than that of the sender.

Sender	Name: 김은희 Address: 서울특별시 광진구 자양동 211번지 은마아파트 201동 502호 Zip Code: 148-204
Recipient	Name: 박진우 Address: 대구광역시 남구 대명동 123번지 Zip Code: 192-143

Reading Practice

(1) 어떻게 지내셨습니까?
How have you been?

(2) 다섯 시까지 오세요.
Please come by 5:00.

(3) 6월 21일에 혜영이의 결혼식이 있습니다.
We'll have Hyeyeoung's wedding ceremony on June 21st.

(4) 연락을 기다리겠습니다.
I'll be waiting for your reply.

(5) 만날 수 있기를 바랍니다.
I look forward to meeting you.

제 17 과

Lesson 17

어디가 아프십니까? Where Does It Hurt?

Key Sentences

1. 등이 아파서 움직일 수가 없습니다. I cannot move because of back pain.
   deung-i apaseo umjigil suga eopsseumnida
2. 금방 나아지겠습니까? Will I be well soon?
   geumbang naajigetseumnikka

Dialogs

Dialog 1

119대원: 119 구조대입니다. This is 119 emergency.
il-il-gu gujodaeimnida

푸 휘: 계단에서 넘어졌는데 움직일 수가 없습니다.
gyedaneseo neomeojyeotneunde umjigil suga eopseumnida
I fell down some stairs and I can't move.

도와 주세요. Please help me.
dowajuseyo

119대원: 주소와 전화 번호를 천천히 말씀해 주십시오.
jusowa jeonhwa beonhoreul cheoncheonhi malsseumhae jusipsio
Please tell me the address and telephone number slowly.

푸 휘: 주소는 강남구 신사동 11번지이고,
jusoneun gangnam-gu sinsa-dong sibilbeonjiigo
The address is 11 Sinsa-dong, Gangnam-gu,

전화 번호는 511-2936입니다.
jeonhwa beonhoneun o-il-il-i-gu-sam-yukimnida
and the telephone number is 511-2936.

119대원: 예, 알겠습니다. 곧 가겠습니다.
ye algetseumnida got gagetseumnida
Yes, I see. We will be there immediately.

Dialog 2 (병원에서) (In the hospital)
byeongwoneseo

의 사: 어디가 아프십니까? Where does it hurt?
eodiga apeusimnikka

푸 휘: 등이 아파서 움직일 수가 없습니다.
deungi apaseo umjigil suga eopsseumnida
I cannot move because of back pain.

의 사: 찜질약을 매일 등에 붙이십시오.
jjimjilyageul maeil deunge buchisipsio
Apply this medicated patch on your back every day.
진통제는 식사 후에 드세요.
jintongjeneun siksa hue deuseyo
Take the painkiller after a meal.

푸 휘: 금방 나아지겠습니까? Will I get well soon?
geumbang naajigetseumnikka

의 사: 3, 4일이면 나아질 거라고 생각합니다.
sam, sailimyeon naajil georago saeng-gakhamnida
I think you will get well in 3 or 4 days.
하지만, 심한 운동은 하지 마십시오.
hajiman, simhan undong-eun haji masipsio
But don't do any strenuous exercises.

푸 휘: 예, 감사합니다. Yes, thank you.
ye, gamsahamnida

▪ Vocabulary and Phrases ▪

- 붙이다 to apply/stick
- 식사 후 after meal
- 나아지다 to get well
- 3,4일이면 in 3 or 4 days
- 말(말씀)하다 to say
- 드세요 to eat/take
- 아프다 to hurt
- 움직이다 to move
- 운동 exercise/sports
- ~ 수 없다 cannot do
- 천천히 slowly
- 생각하다 to think about
- 진찰 diagnosis
- 등 back
- 매일 every day
- 하지만 but
- 하다 to do
- 돕다 to help
- 심한 severe/extreme
- 찜질약 medicated patch
- 넘어지다 to fall down
- 어디 where
- 마십시오 don't do
- 주소 address
- ~ 후 after
- 가겠습니다 will go
- 계단 stairs/stairway
- 금방(곧) soon
- 말씀해 주세요 please say
- 119구조대 119 emergency
- 전화 번호 phone number
- 나아질 거라고 may get well
- 진통제 painkiller/pain reliever
- 도와 주세요 please give (me some) help

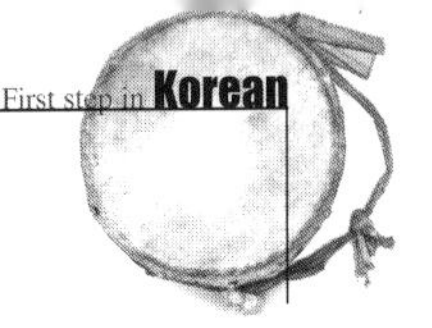

Word Drills

Symptoms of disease

목이 아프다 mogi apeuda
sore throat

머리가 아프다 meoriga apeuda
headache

열이 있다 yeori itda
fever

이가 아프다 iga apeuda
toothache

피부가 가렵다 pibuga garyeopda
skin itch

콧물이 나다 konmuri nada
runny nose

주사를 놓다 jusareul nota
shot

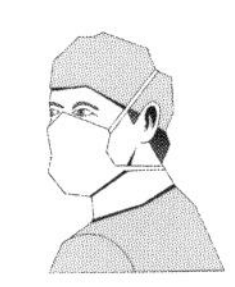

수술하다 susulhada
to operate

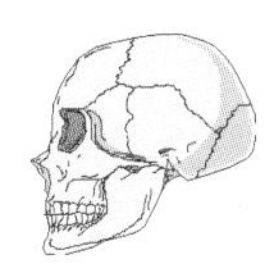

엑스레이를 찍다 eks-reireul jjikda
to take an X-ray

Structures and Expressions

1. The casual connective '～서' expresses the cause of the first verb. And '～수(가) 없습니다' means 'cannot do'.

> **등이 아파서 움직일 수가 없습니다.**
> : I cannot move because I feel pain in my back.

머리가 아파서 걸어갈 수가 없습니다.
meoriga apaseo georeogal suga eopsseumnida
I cannot walk because I have a headache.

목이 아파서 밥을 먹을 수가 없습니다.
mogi apaseo babeul meogeul suga eopsseumnida
I cannot eat because I have a sore throat.

콧물이 나서 공부할 수가 없습니다.
konmuri naseo gongbuhal suga eopsseumnida
I cannot study because I have a runny nose.

늦게 자서 일어날 수가 없습니다.
neutge jaseo ireonal suga eopsseumnida
I cannot get up because I went to bed late.

② The construction '~(으)ㄹ거라고 생각합니다' expresses the speaker's guess or idea.

> **3, 4일이면 나아질 거라고 생각합니다.**
> : I think that I will get well in 3 or 4 days.

그는 한국어를 공부할 거라고 생각합니다.
geuneun hangugeoreul gongbuhal georago saenggakhamnida
I think he will study Korean.

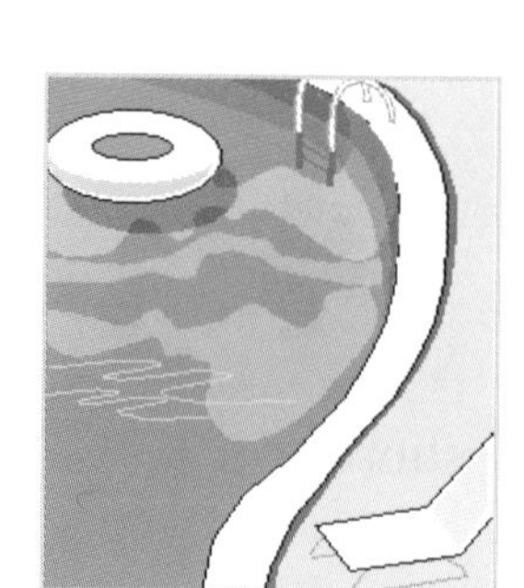

그는 내일 결석할 거라고 생각합니다.
geuneun naeil gyeolseokhal georago saenggakhamnida
I think he may be absent tomorrow.

그는 이번 주까지 올 거라고 생각합니다.
geuneun ibeon jukkaji ol georago saenggakhamnida
I think he will be back by this week.

그는 수영장에서 수영할 거라고 생각합니다.
geuneun suyeongjang-eseo suyeonghal georago saenggakhamnida
I think he may swim in the swimming pool.

그는 곧 나아질 거라고 생각합니다.
geuneun got naajil georago saenggakhamnida
I think he will get well soon.

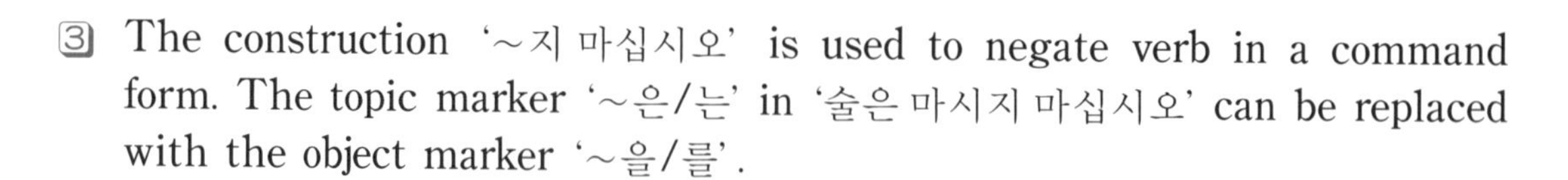

③ The construction '~지 마십시오' is used to negate verb in a command form. The topic marker '~은/는' in '술은 마시지 마십시오' can be replaced with the object marker '~을/를'.

> **심한 운동은 하지 마십시오.**
> : Don't do any strenuous exercises.

술은 마시지 마십시오.
sureun masiji masipsio
Please do not drink alcohol.

결석은 하지 마십시오.
gyeolseogeun haji masipsio
Please do not skip the class.

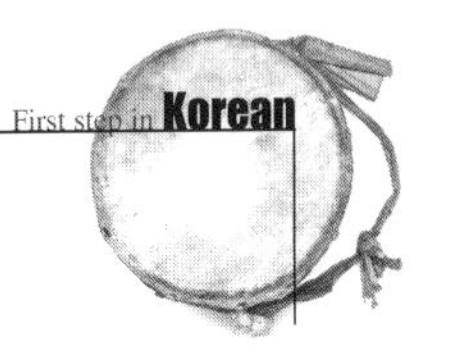

담배는 피우지 마십시오.
dambaeneun piuji masipsio
Please do not smoke.

④ '～고(and)' is used in the following cases for two or more simple sentences.

저는 나이지리아 사람이고, 친구는 한국 사람입니다.
jeoneun naijiria saramigo chin-guneun hanguk saramimnida
I am a Nigerian and my friend is a Korean.

저는 도서관에 가고, 친구는 식당에 갑니다.
jeoneun doseogwane gago chin-guneun sikdang-e gamnida
I go to the library and my friend goes to the restaurant.

⑤ The future tense marker '～겠' is used for the future tense.

금방 나아지겠습니까?
geumbang naajigetseumnikka
Will I get well soon?

내일 전화하겠습니다.
naeil jeonhwahagetseumnida
I will call tomorrow.

⑥ The connective '～는데' makes two clauses conjoined in such a way that the action taking place in the first sentence still continues in the second sentence.

넘어졌는데 움직일 수가 없습니다.
neomeojyeonneunde umjigil suga eopsseumnida
I fell down and can't move.

공부하는데 조용히 하십시오.
gongbuhaneunde joyonghi hasipsio
Please be quiet because I'm studying.

Exercises

1 Change the sentences as shown in the examples.

(1)

Example
허리가 아프다. → 허리가 아파서 공부할 수가 없습니다.

① 열이 있다. → ______________________

② 목이 아프다. → ____________________

③ 기침이 나다. → ____________________

④ 콧물이 나다. → ____________________

⑤ 머리가 아프다. → ____________________

(2)

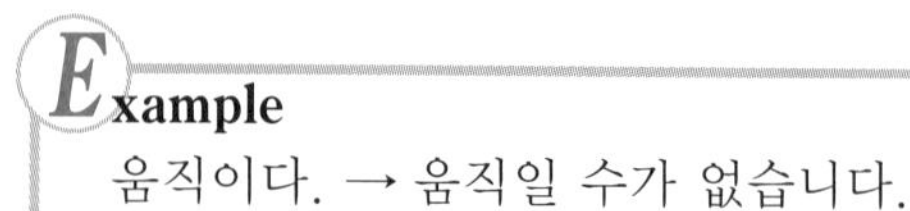

Example
움직이다. → 움직일 수가 없습니다.

① 밥을 먹다. → __________　　② 잠을 자다. → __________

③ 운동을 하다. → __________　　④ 일찍 일어나다. → __________

⑤ 술을 마시다. → __________

2 Provide answers for the following questions and discuss them.

(1) 금방 나아지겠습니까? Will I get well soon?

(2) 언제, 왜 갔었습니까? When and why did you go there?

(3) 어디가 아팠습니까? Where did it hurt?

(4) 의사 선생님은 무슨 말씀을 하셨습니까? What did the doctor say?

Reading Practice

(1) 계단에서 넘어져 119 구조대에 전화를 걸었습니다.
I've called 119 emergency because I fell down some stairs.

(2) 주소와 전화 번호를 말씀해 주세요.
Please tell me the address and telephone number.

(3) 다리가 아파서 움직일 수가 없습니다.
I can't move because my leg hurts.

(4) 의사가 진통제를 주었습니다.
The doctor prescribed some painkiller.

(5) 3, 4일이면 나아질 거라고 했습니다.
The doctor told me I will get better in 3 or 4 days.

제 18 과

Lesson 18

무슨 운동을 좋아하십니까?
What Sports Do You Like?

Key Sentences

1. 테니스는 좋아하지 않지만, 수영은 좋아합니다.
tenisneun joahaji anchiman suyeong-eun joahamnida
I don't like tennis, but I like swimming.

2. 무슨 음료수를 좋아하십니까? What do you like to drink?
museun eumryosureul joahasimnikka

Dialogs

Dialog 1

푸휘: 어제는 무엇을 하셨습니까?
eojeneun mueoseul hasyeotseumnikka
What did you do yesterday?

영주: 운동과 쇼핑을 했습니다.
undonggwa syoping-eul haetseumnida
I did some exercise and went shopping.

푸휘: 무슨 운동을 좋아하십니까?
museun undong-eul joahasimnikka
What kind of sports do you like?

영주: 테니스를 좋아합니다. I like tennis.
teniseureul joahamnida

푸휘 씨는 어떻습니까? Puhui, how about you?
puhwi ssineun eotteoseumnikka

푸휘: 저는 테니스는 좋아하지 않지만, 수영은 좋아합니다.
jeoneun tenisneun joahaji anchiman suyeong-eun joahamnida
I don't like tennis, but I like swimming.

영주: 저도 수영을 좋아하니까, 이번 주말에 수영하러 같이 가지 않겠습니까?
jeodo suyeong-eul joahanikka ibeon jumale suyeonghareo gachi gaji anketseumnikka
I also like swimming, so wouldn't you like to go swimming together this weekend?

푸휘: 예, 좋습니다. Yes, that will be good.
ye jossumnida

Dialog 2 (수영장에서) (At the swimming pool)
suyeongjang-eseo

영주: 푸휘 씨는 정말로 수영을 잘 하시는군요.
puhwi ssineun jeongmallo suyeong-eul jal hasineun-gunyo
Puhui, you swim very well.

이제 음료수를 마시러 가지 않겠습니까?
ije eumryosureul masireo gaji anketseumnikka
Wouldn't you like to go and get something to drink?

푸휘: 그렇게 합시다. Let's do that.
geureoke hapsida

무슨 음료를 좋아합니까? What would you like to drink?
museun eumryoreul joahamnikka

영주: 오렌지 주스, 사이다, 콜라는 좋아합니다만, 커피는 좋아하지 않습니다.
orenji jus saida kollaneun joahamnidaman keopineun joahaji ansseumnida
I like orange juice, sprite, and cola, but I don't like coffee.

푸휘: 저도 커피는 싫어합니다. I also dislike coffee.
jeodo keopineun sireohamnida

영주: 저기에 자판기가 있습니다.
jeogie japangiga itseumnida
There is a vending machine over there.

Vocabulary and Phrases

- 어제 yesterday
- 무슨 what
- 테니스 tennis
- 저 I
- 정말로 really
- 음료수 drinks
- 사이다 sprite
- 저기에 over there
- 좋습니다 I like it / okay
- 있다 there is
- 수영하러 to swim
- 싫어하다 to dislike
- 쇼핑 shopping
- 좋아하다 to like
- 않다 not
- 이번에 this time
- 잘 well
- 마시다 to drink
- 콜라 cola
- 커피 coffee
- 무엇을 what
- 좋아하지 않지만 I don't like it, but
- 마실 것 something to drink
- 가지 않겠습니까? Won't you go?
- 어떻습니까? how about …?
- 수영 swimming
- 주말 weekend
- 같이 with/together
- 이제 now
- 그렇게 so
- 오렌지 주스 orange juice
- 좋아합니다만 I like it, but
- 자판기 vending machine

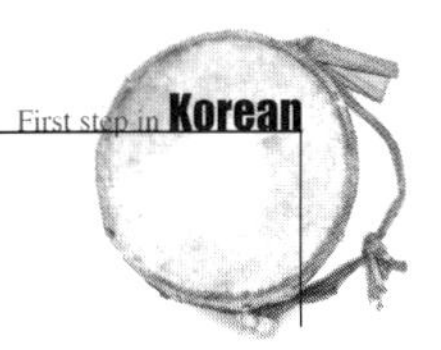

Word Drills

Sport

농구를 하다
nong-gureul hada
to play basketball

축구를 하다
chuk-gureul hada
to play soccer

야구를 하다
yagureul hada
to play baseball

테니스를 치다
teniseureul chida
to play tennis

골프를 치다
golpeureul chida
to play golf

스키를 타다
skireul tada
to ski

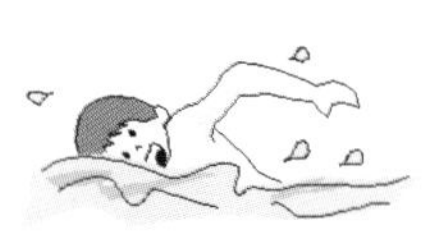

수영을 하다
suyeong-eul hada
to swim

태권도를 하다
taegwondoreul hada
to do Taegwondo

Structures and Expressions

1. When you ask about what kinds of things someone likes, use the question word '무슨'. Note that '무슨' is an adjective, while '무엇' belongs to the functional category, noun.

무슨 운동을 좋아하십니까? What kind of sports do you like?	**무엇을 좋아하십니까?** What do you like?

무슨 요리를 좋아하십니까?
museun yorireul joahasimnikka
What kind of food do you like?

무슨 음악을 좋아하십니까?
museun eumageul joahasimnikka
What kind of music do you like?

무슨 색을 좋아하십니까?
museun saegeul joahasimnikka
What kind of color do you like?

무슨 과일을 좋아하십니까?
museun gwaireul joahasimnikka
What kind of fruit do you like?

2. When you want to express that you like something, use the expression '~을/를 좋아합니다'.

수영을 좋아합니다. : I like swimming.

야구하는 것을 좋아합니다.
yaguhaneun geoseul joahamnida
I like to play baseball.

태권도하는 것을 좋아합니다.
taegwondohaneun geoseul joahamnida
I like to do Taegwondo.

스키 타는 것을 좋아합니다.
ski taneun geoseul joahamnida
I like to ski.

테니스 치는 것을 좋아합니다.
teniseu chineun geoseul joahamnida
I like to play tennis.

탁구 치는 것을 좋아합니다. I like to play table tennis.
takgu chineun geoseul joahamnida

③ '~지만' expresses the idea 'although' or 'but', attached to the verb of a first clause. Its negative form is '~지 않지만'.

수영은 좋아하지만, : Although I like swimming,
수영은 좋아하지 않지만, : Although I don't like swimming,

수영은 좋아하지 않지만, 테니스는 좋아합니다.
suyeong-eun joahaji anchiman teniseuneun joahamnida
I don't like swimming, but I like to play tennis.

영화는 좋아하지만, 음악은 좋아하지 않습니다.
yeonghwaneun joahajiman eumageun joahaji ansseumnida
I like movies, but I don't like music.

④ '~지 않겠습니까?' expresses the idea 'won't you?'.

주말에 테니스 치러 가지 않겠습니까?
: Won't you play tennis this weekend?

골프 치러 가지 않겠습니까?
golpeuchireo gaji anketseumnikka
Won't you play golf?

영화 보러 가지 않겠습니까?
yeonghwa boreo gaji anketseumnikka
Won't you go to the movies?

식사하러 가지 않겠습니까?
siksahareo gaji anketseumnikka
Won't you eat dinner?

5 Attached to a verb stem, the connective '(으)러' indicates 'purpose' or 'goal' of an action.

> **수영하러 갑니다.** : I go to swim.
> **주스를 마시러 갑니다.** : I go to drink orange juice.

레스토랑에 점심을 먹으러 갑니다. I go to a restaurant to have lunch.
restorang-e jeomsimeul meogeureo gamnida

도서관에 공부를 하러 갑니다. I go to a library to study.
doseogwane gongbureul hareo gamnida

6 '~(으)니까' expresses the idea that the action stated in the first clause is a reason for the second clause.

> **수영을 좋아하니까, 같이 가겠습니다.**
> : Because I like swimming, I will go there with (you).

한국에서 살았으니까, 한국말을 잘합니다.
hangugeseo sarasseunikka hangukmareul jalhamnida
Because I've lived in Korea, I can speak Korean well.

Exercises

1 Write Korean words in the blanks as shown in the example.

> **Example**
> school (학교)

(1) like (　　)　(2) swimming (　　)　(3) dislike (　　)
(4) do well (　　)　(5) sport (　　)　(6) tennis (　　)

2 Complete the sentences following the example.

> **Example**
> 테니스, 수영 → 테니스는 좋아하지 않지만, 수영은 좋아합니다.

(1) 커피, 주스 → ____________________

(2) 사과, 바나나 → ____________________

(3) 야구, 농구 → ____________________

(4) 쓰기, 읽기 → ____________________

(5) 라면, 자장면 → ____________________

3 Make sentences of suggestion following the example.

> **Example**
> 골프 치다. → 골프 치러 갑시다.

(1) 밥을 먹다. → ____________________

(2) 영화 보다. → ____________________

(3) 커피를 마시다. → ____________________

(4) 수영을 하다. → ____________________

(5) 한국어를 공부하다. → ____________________

4 Provide an answer for the following questions and discuss them.

(1) 무슨 운동을 좋아하십니까? What sport do you like?

(2) 좋아하는 운동은 무엇입니까? What is your favorite sport?

(3) 무슨 운동을 잘하십니까? What sport do you play well?

(4) 무슨 음료를 좋아하십니까? What do you like to drink?

Reading Practice

(1) 어제는 운동과 쇼핑을 했습니다.
Yesterday, I played some sports and went shopping.

(2) 저는 농구를 좋아하지만, 테니스는 좋아하지 않습니다.
I like basketball, but I don't like tennis.

(3) 무슨 음료수를 드시겠습니까?
What kind of beverage would you like to drink?

(4) 영주 씨와 저는 커피를 싫어합니다.
Yeoungju and I dislike coffee.

(5) 주말에 탁구장에 같이 가지 않겠습니까?
Why don't we go to the table tennis center together on the weekend?

제 19 과

Lesson 19

세탁물을 맡기려고 합니다.

I'm Going to Have My Laundry Drycleaned.

Key Sentences

1. 재킷을 세탁하려고 합니다. I'd like to have the jacket drycleaned.
   jaekiseul setakharyeogo hamnida
2. 금요일 오후까지 배달해 드리겠습니다. I will deliver it by Friday afternoon.
   geumyoil ohukkaji baedalhae deurigetseumnida

Dialogs

Dialog 1

영주: 푸휘 씨, 재킷이 아주 멋있군요.
puhwi ssi jaekisi aju meoditgunyo
Puhui, your jacket is nice.

푸휘: 어제 남대문 시장에서 샀습니다.
eoje namdaemun sijang-eseo satseumnida
I bought it at the Namdaemun market yesterday.

영주: 그런데, 재킷에 무엇이 묻었군요.
geureonde jaekise mueosi mudeotgunyo
By the way, your jacket has a stain on it.

푸휘: 이런! 사자마자 더러워졌군요. 어떻게 하면 좋겠습니까?
ireon sajamaja deoreowojyeotgunyo otteoke hamyeon joketseumnikka
Oh, no! It got dirty as soon as I bought it. What should I do?

영주: 옆 건물 2층에 세탁소가 있습니다. 같이 갈까요?
yeop geonmul icheung-e setaksoga isseumnida gachi galkkayo
There is a drycleaner's in the next building on the 2nd floor. Should I go with you?

푸휘: 아니오, 괜찮습니다. No, it's okay.
anio gwaenchanseumnida
혼자 갈 수 있습니다. I can go by myself.
honja gal su itseumnida

Dialog 2 (세탁소에서) (At the drycleaner's)
setaksoeseo

푸휘: 실례합니다. 이 재킷을 세탁하려고 합니다.
sillyehamnida i jaekiseul setakharyeogo hamnida
Excuse me. I'd like to have this jacket drycleaned.

세탁소 주인: 이런! 많이 더러워졌군요.
ireon mani deoreowojyeotgunyo
Oh, no! It's really dirty.

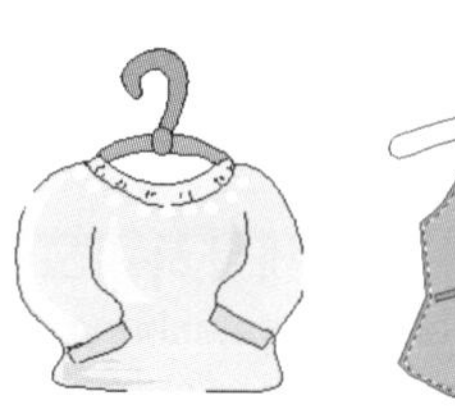

무엇이 묻었습니까?
mueosi mudeotseumnikka
What's the stain?

푸휘: 모르겠어요. 어제 샀는데…
moreugesseoyo eoje sanneunde...
I don't know. I bought it yesterday.

세탁비는 얼마입니까?
setakbineun eolmaimnikka
How much is the drycleaning fee?

세탁소 주인: 재킷은 6,000원입니다.
jaekiseun yukcheonwonimnida
A jacket is 6,000 won.

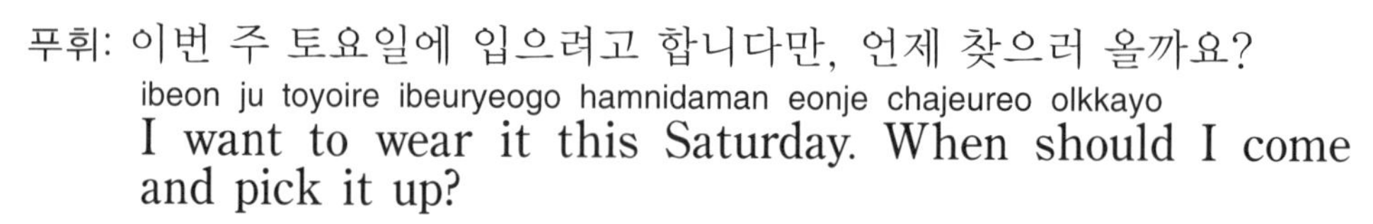

푸휘: 이번 주 토요일에 입으려고 합니다만, 언제 찾으러 올까요?
ibeon ju toyoire ibeuryeogo hamnidaman eonje chajeureo olkkayo
I want to wear it this Saturday. When should I come and pick it up?

세탁소 주인: 금요일 오후까지 배달해 드리겠습니다.
geumyoil ohukkaji baedalhae deurigetseumnida
I'll have it delivered by Friday afternoon.

푸휘: 감사합니다. Thank you.
gamsahamnida

Vocabulary and Phrases

- 재킷 jacket
- 어제 yesterday
- 배달하다 to deliver
- 더러워지다 to get dirty
- 2층 second floor
- 괜찮습니다 it is ok
- 아주 very
- 사다 to buy
- 그런데 by the way
- 옆 next
- 세탁소 drycleaner's
- 혼자 alone
- 멋있다 fashionable/nice
- 묻다 to stain
- 이런 Oh, no!
- 건물 building
- 같이 with
- 많이 a lot

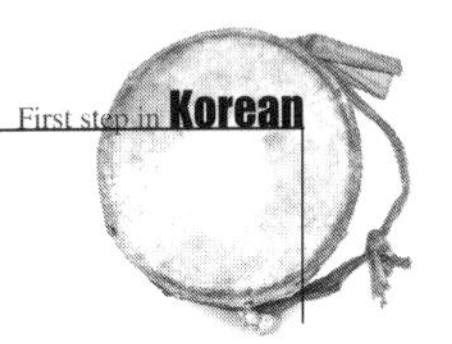

- 언제 when
- 금요일 Friday
- 찾다 to get (it) back/find
- 입다 to wear (clothes)
- 실례합니다 excuse me
- 모르다 don't know
- 감사합니다 thank you
- 사자마자 right after I bought (it)
- ~만 but
- 주인 owner
- 세탁비 drycleaning fee
- 토요일 Saturday
- 세탁하려고 to dryclean
- 배달해 드리다 to have (it) delivered
- 남대문 시장 Namdaemun market
- 이번 주 this week
- 오후 afternoon

Word Drills

세탁을 하다
setageul hada
to have (it) drycleaned

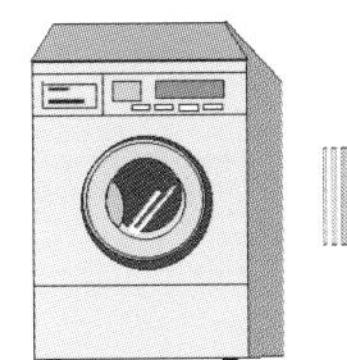

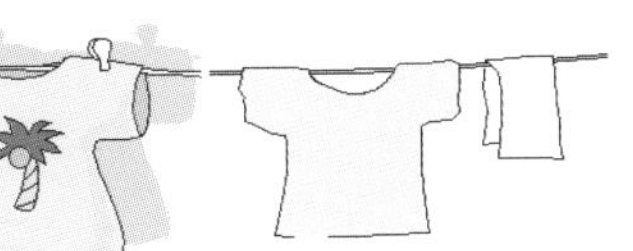

다림질을 하다
darimjireul hada
to iron

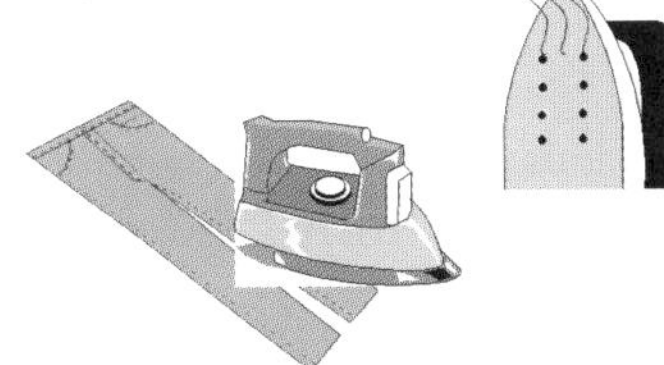

바짓단을 줄이다
bajitdaneul jurida
to have the pants shortened

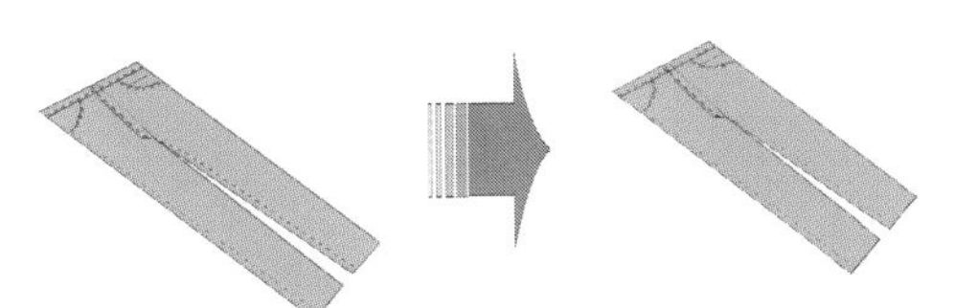

허릿단을 늘리다
heoritdaneul neullida
to let out the waist

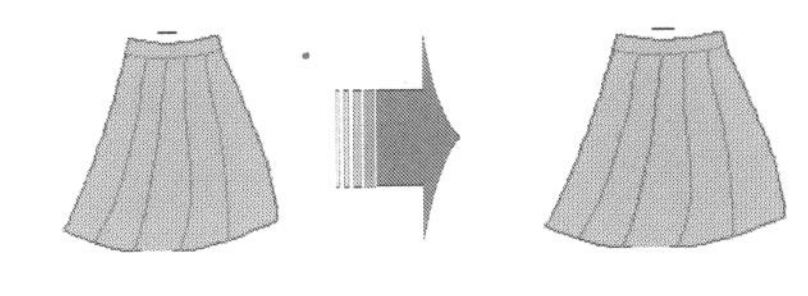

Structures and Expressions

① The expression '~자마자' expresses the idea of 'as soon as' or 'right after'. The second action follows immediately after the first action.

> **사자마자** : right after I bought it

밥을 먹자마자 회사에 갔습니다.
babeul meokjamaja hoesae gatseumnida
Right after I finished eating, I went to work.

일어나자마자 학교에 갔습니다.
ireonajamaja hakgyoe gatseumnida
As soon as I got up, I went to school.

집에 가자마자 친구에게 전화했습니다.
jibe gajamaja chinguege jeonhwahaetseumnida
As soon as I got home, I made a phone call.

② The expression '~(으)려고 합니다' expresses the idea of 'plan to do'.

이 재킷을 세탁하려고 합니다.
: I plan to (would like to) dry clean this jacket.

무슨 운동을 하려고 합니까?
museun undong-eul haryeogo hamnikka
What sports are you planning to do?

한국어를 공부하려고 합니다.
hangugeoreul gongbuharyeogo hamnida
I'm planning to study Korean.

친구를 만나려고 합니다.
chin-gureul mannaryeogo hamnida
I'm planning to meet my friend.

양복을 맡기려고 합니다.
yangbogeul matgiryeogo hamnida
I'm planning to have my suit tailored.

③ The expression '~까지' is a postposition, meaning 'to', 'up to', 'until', or 'by'.

수요일까지 숙제를 제출하겠습니다.
: I will hand in my homework by Wednesday.

수원까지 40분 걸립니다. It takes 40 minutes to Suwon.
suwonkkaji sasipbun geollimnida

도서관까지 걸어갔습니다. I walked to the library.
doseogwankkaji georeogatsemnida

밤 늦게까지 책을 읽었습니다. I read books until late night.
bam neukkekkaji chaegeul ilgeotseumnida

4시까지 한국어를 공부합니다. I study Korean till 4 o'clock.
nesikkaji hangugeoreul gongbuhamnida

Exercises

1 Make sentences using the future tense marker '겠' following the example below.

Example

세탁물을 맡기다 → 세탁물을 맡기겠습니다.

leave the laundry → I would like to leave my laundry.

(1) 양복을 사다 to buy a suit → ____________

(2) 세탁소에 가다 to go to the drycleaner's → ____________

(3) 선물을 배달하다 to deliver the gift → ____________

(4) 토요일에 찾다 to pick (it) up on Saturday → ____________

(5) 같이 가다 to go together → ____________

2 Rewrite the sentences following the examples.

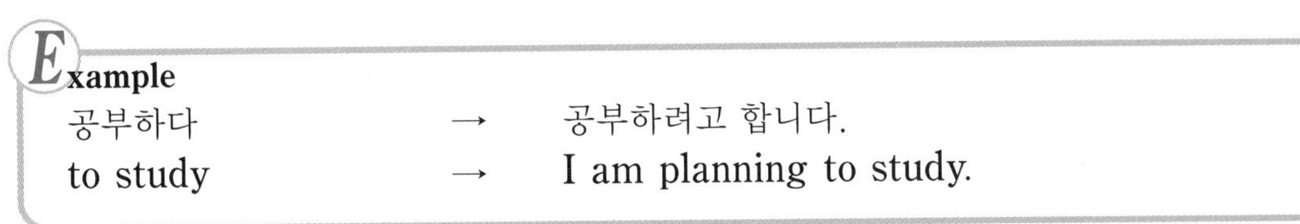

Example

공부하다 → 공부하려고 합니다.

to study → I am planning to study.

(1) 커피를 마시다 drink coffee → ____________

(2) 수영을 하다 swim → ____________

(3) 세탁물을 맡기다 leave the laundry → ____________

(4) 일찍 자다 to sleep early → ____________

3 Rewrite the sentences following the example below.

Example

파티가 끝나다/세탁소에 가다 → 파티가 끝나자마자 세탁소에 갔습니다.

As soon as the party ended, I went to the drycleaner's.

(1) 우유를 마시다/운동을 하다

→ ____________________________

(2) 양복을 사다/세탁하다

→ ______________________________

(3) 수업이 끝나다/식당에 가다

→ ______________________________

(4) 일찍 일어나다/회사에 가다

→ ______________________________

4 Provide answers for the questions and discuss them.

(1) 세탁소에 간 적이 있습니까?
Have you ever been to the drycleaner's?

(2) 무엇을 했습니까?
What did you do?

(3) 세탁비는 양복 한 벌에 얼마입니까?
How much is the drycleaning fee for a suit?

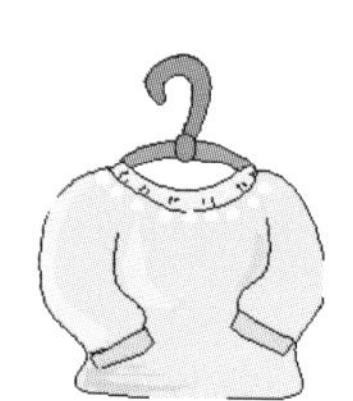

Reading Practice

(1) 어제는 백화점에서 재킷을 샀습니다.
Yesterday, I bought the jacket at a department store.

(2) 세탁비는 얼마입니까?
How much is the drycleaning fee?

(3) 언제 찾으러 올까요?
When should I come and pick it up?

(4) 투피스 한 벌에 6,000원입니다.
One two-piece suit is 6,000 won.

(5) 금요일 오후까지 배달해 드리겠습니다.
I'll have it delivered by Friday afternoon.

제 20 과
Lesson 20

편지를 쓰고 있습니다.
I'm Writing a Letter.

Key Sentences

1. 부모님께 편지를 쓰고 있습니다. I'm writing a letter to my parents.
   bumonimkke pyeonjireul sseugo itseumnida
2. 이 편지를 중국으로 부치려고 합니다. I'd like to send this letter to China.
   i pyeonjireul jung-gugeuro buchiryeogo hamnida

Dialogs

Dialog 1

영주: 무엇을 하고 있습니까?
mueoseul hago itseumnikka
What are you doing?

푸휘: 편지를 쓰고 있습니다.
pyeonjireul sseugo itseumnida
I'm writing a letter.

영주: 누구에게 쓰고 있습니까?
nuguege sseugo itseumnikka
Who are you writing to?

푸휘: 부모님께 쓰고 있습니다.
bumonimkke sseugo itseumnida
I'm writing a letter to my parents.

그런데 봉투는 어떻게 씁니까?
geureonde bongtuneun eotteoke sseumnikka
But how do you write on the envelope?

영주: 앞면 중간 부분에 받을 사람의 주소와 이름을 쓰고,
apmyeon junggan bubune badeul saramui jusowa ireumeul sseugo
You write the recipient's address on the front middle,

30 74
보내는 사람 (빠른우편표시) (우표첨부)
주소, 성명, 우편번호 기재
※발송인이 필요한 사항 기재가능
40
90 ~ 120
(우체국사용란)
등기취급시 접수국
등기번호표시
※이용자는 기재 불가
받는 사람
주소, 성명, 우편번호기재
※발송인이 필요한 사항 기재가능
□□□-□□□
※이 간격을 지키지 않으면 규격외 봉투로 간주되어 추가요금부담
140~235
(각 부분 기재위치는 ±5mm까지 가능)

왼쪽 윗부분에 보내는 사람의 주소와 이름을 씁니다.
oenjjok witbubune bonaeneun saramui jusowa ireumeul sseumnida
and you write the sender's address on the upper left.

푸휘: 소포를 부치려면 우체국에 가야 됩니까?
soporeul buchiryeomyeon ucheguge gaya doemnikka
If I send a parcel, do I have to go to the post office?

영주: 예, 직접 가셔야 됩니다.
ye jikjeop gasyeoya doemnida
Yes, you have to go there in person.

Dialog 2 (우체국에서) (At the post office)
uchegugeseo

푸휘: 이 편지를 중국으로 부치려고 합니다.
i pyeonjireul jung-gugeuro buchiryeogo hamnida
I'd like to send this letter to China.

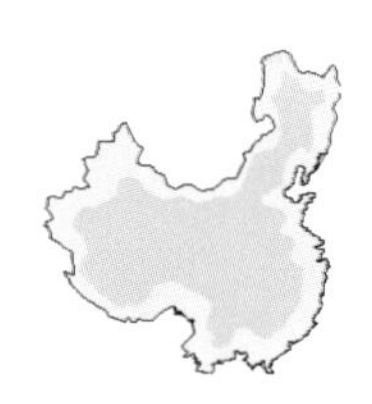

직원: 360원입니다. It's 360 won.
sambaek-yuksip wonimnida

푸휘: 이 소포도 부쳐 주십시오.
i sopodo buchyeo jusipsio
Please send this parcel, too.

직원: 4,200원입니다. It's 4,200 won.
sacheonibaek wonimnida

깨지는 물건은 아닙니까?
kkaejineun mulgeoneun animnikka
Isn't it fragile?

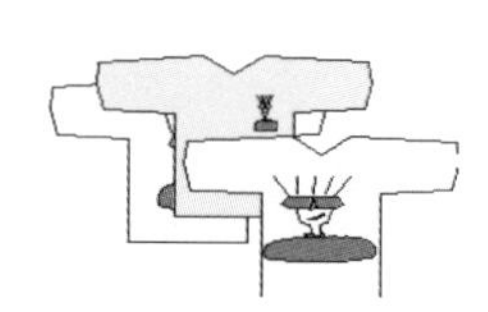

푸휘: 예, 티셔츠와 손수건입니다.
ye tisyeocheuwa sonsugeonimnida
No, they are T-shirts and handkerchiefs.

그런데, 어느 정도 걸립니까?
geureonde eoneu jeongdo geolrimnikka
By the way, how long will it take?

직원: 요즈음은 바빠서 1주일에서 10일 정도 걸립니다.
yojeueumeun bappaseo iljuireseo sibil jeongdo geolrimnida
Since it is busy, it will take about one week to 10 days.

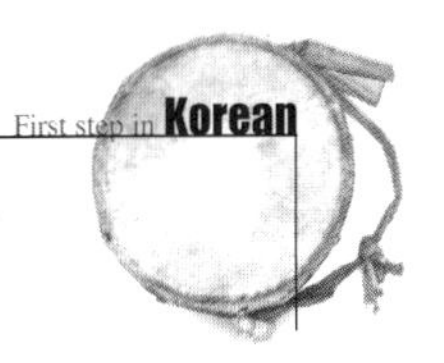

Vocabulary and Phrases

- 하다 to do
- 쓰고 있다 is writing
- 받을 사람 recipient
- 우체국 post office
- 물건 things/items
- 티셔츠 T-shirt
- 요즈음 these days
- 부모님 parents
- 중간부분 in the middle
- 보내는 사람 sender
- 직접 in person
- 바쁘다 to be busy
- ~정도 about/degree
- 편지 letter
- 부모님께 to parents
- 윗부분 on the top
- 가야 되다 must go
- 부쳐 주다 to send
- 어느 정도 about how long
- 하고 있다 is doing
- 그런데 by the way
- 주소 address
- 부치다 to send
- 아닙니까? Isn't it?
- 걸리다 to take
- 바빠서 since it is busy
- 봉투 envelope
- 앞면 front
- 이름 name
- 소포 parcel
- 중국 China
- 달다 to weigh
- 쓰다 to write
- 어떻게 how
- 왼쪽 left
- 가다 to go
- 손수건 handkerchief
- 깨지다 to be fragile

Word Drills

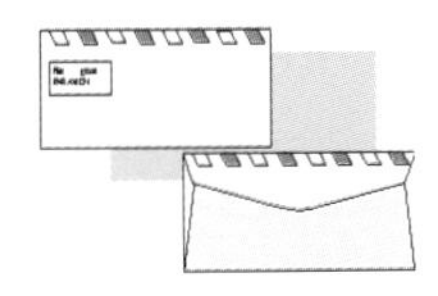

국제우편 international mail
gukjeupyeon

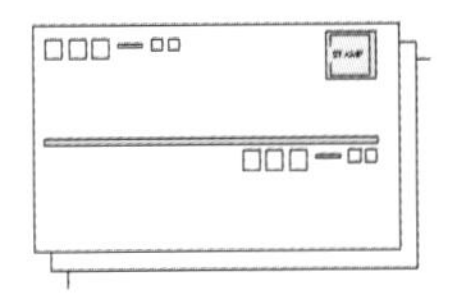

국내우편 domestic mail
guknaeupyeon

소포 parcel
sopo

빠른우편 express
ppareunupyeon

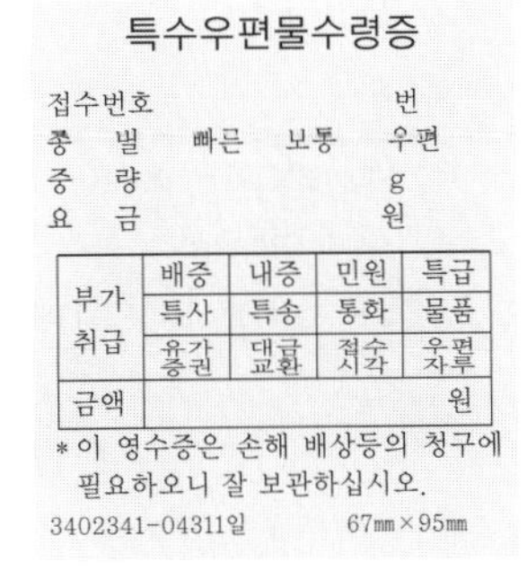

특수우편물수령증

접수번호 번
종 별 빠른 보통 우편
중 량 g
요 금 원

부가취급	배증	내증	민원	특급
	특사	특송	통화	물품
	유가증권	대금교환	접수시각	우편자루
금액				원

* 이 영수증은 손해 배상등의 청구에 필요하오니 잘 보관하십시오.

3402341-04311일 67㎜×95㎜

등기 registered
deunggi

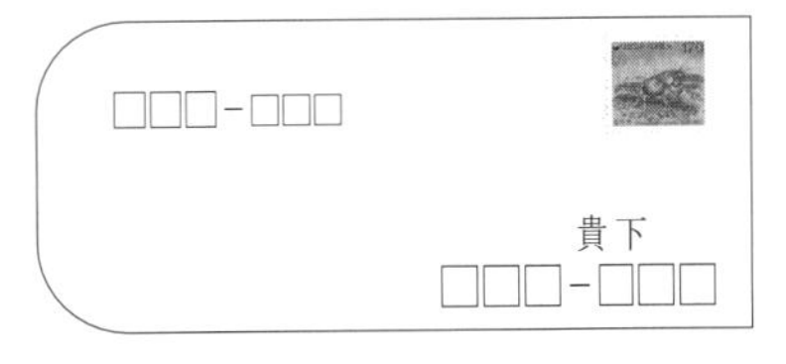

보통우편 regular mail
botongupyeon

Structures and Expressions

① The sentence ending '~고 있습니다' is a progressive verb form like 'being' in English, indicating that an action is in progress.

편지를 쓰고 있습니다. : I'm writing a letter.

한국어를 공부하고 있습니다.
hangugeoreul gongbuhago itseumnida
I'm studying Korean.

중국어 숙제를 하고 있습니다.
junggugeo sukjereul hago itseumnida
I'm doing my Chinese homework.

소포를 부치고 있습니다.
soporeul buchigo itseumnida
I'm sending a parcel.

② The sentence connective '~고' makes two clauses conjoined in a equal status, meaning 'and'.

동생은 공부하고, 나는 편지를 씁니다.
: My brother is studying and I am writing a letter.

친구는 밥을 먹고, 나는 빵을 먹습니다.
chin-guneun babeul meokgo naneun ppang-eul meoksseumnida
My friend is eating steamed rice and I am eating bread.

친구는 10시에 자고, 나는 12시에 잡니다.
chin-guneun yeolsie jago naneun yeoldusie jamnida
My friend goes to bed at 10 and I go to bed at 12.

영주 씨는 테니스를 좋아하고, 나는 수영을 좋아합니다.
yeongju ssineun teniseureul joahago naneun suyeong-eul joahamnida
Yeongju likes to play tennis and I like to swim.

③ The causal connective '~어/아서' expresses the idea of 'because'.

바빠서 오래 걸립니다. : It takes long because it is busy.

게을러서 늦게 일어납니다.
geeulleoseo neutge ireonamnida
He gets up late because he is lazy.

슬퍼서 울었습니다.
seulpeoseo ureotseumnida
I cried because I was sad.

④ The expression '～정도' conveys the meaning of 'approximately that much (many)'.

학생이 20명 정도입니다. : There are about 20 students.

학교까지 몇 분 정도 걸립니까?
hakgyokkaji myeot bun jeongdo geollimnikka
About how long does it take to go to the school?

⑤ The expression '～면' corresponds to 'if' in English, and '～(으)려면' means 'if (you) plan to (want to) do'.

우체국에 가면 소포를 부칠 수 있습니다.
: If you go to the post office, you can send a parcel.

소포를 부치려면 우체국에 가야 됩니다.
: If you plan to (want to) send a parcel, you should go to a post office.

공부를 하려면 도서관에 가야 합니다.
gongbureul haryeomyeon doseogwane gaya hamnida
If you want to study, you should go to the library.

빨리 달리면 경주에서 이길 수 있습니다.
ppalli dallimyeon gyeongjueseo igil su itseumnida
If you run fast, you will win the race.

Exercises

1 Complete the following dialogs, following the examples.

(1)

Example
편지를 쓰다 → 편지를 쓰려면 어떻게 합니까?

① 소포를 부치다 to send a parcel
→ ______________________

② 우체국에 가다 to go to the post office
→ ______________________

③ 무게를 달다 to weigh
→ ______________________

④ 도서관에 가다 to go to the library
→ ______________________

⑤ 양복을 사다 to buy a suit
→ ______________________

(2)

Example
편지를 쓰다 → 편지를 쓰고 있습니다.

① 무게를 달다 to weigh
→ ______________________

② 전화를 걸다 to make a phone call
→ ______________________

③ 우유를 마시다 to drink milk
→ ______________________

④ 책을 읽다 to read a book
→ ______________________

⑤ 한국어를 공부하다 to study Korean
→ ______________________

2 Fill in '~에게' or '~께' in the blanks.

(1) 친구(　　) 편지를 쓰고 있습니다.
I am writing a letter to my friend.

(2) 할아버지(　　) 전화를 걸었습니다.
I've made a phone call to my grandfather.

(3) 선생님(　　) 소포를 부쳤습니다.
I've sent a parcel to my teacher.

(4) 동생(　　) 선물을 주었습니다.
I've given a present to my brother.

(5) 사장님(　　) 한국어를 가르쳐 드리고 있습니다.
I'm teaching my boss Korean.

3 Provide answers for the questions and discuss them.

(1) 편지 봉투는 어떻게 씁니까?
How do I write on the envelope?

(2) 소포를 부치려면 어떻게 합니까?
How do I send a parcel?

(3) 우체국에 간 적이 있습니까?
Have you ever been to the post office?

(4) 부모님께 편지를 쓴 적이 있습니까?
Have you ever written a letter to your parents?

Reading Practice

(1) 친구에게 편지를 쓰고 있습니다.
I'm writing a letter to my friend.

(2) 부모님께 엽서를 쓰고 있습니다.
I'm writing a postcard to my parents.

(3) 오늘 우체국에서 편지와 소포를 부쳤습니다.
I sent the letter and the parcel at the post office today.

(4) 깨지는 물건은 아닙니까?
Isn't it fragile?

(5) 이 편지를 미얀마에 부치려고 합니다.
I'd like to send this letter to Myanmar.

한국 지도
Map of Korea

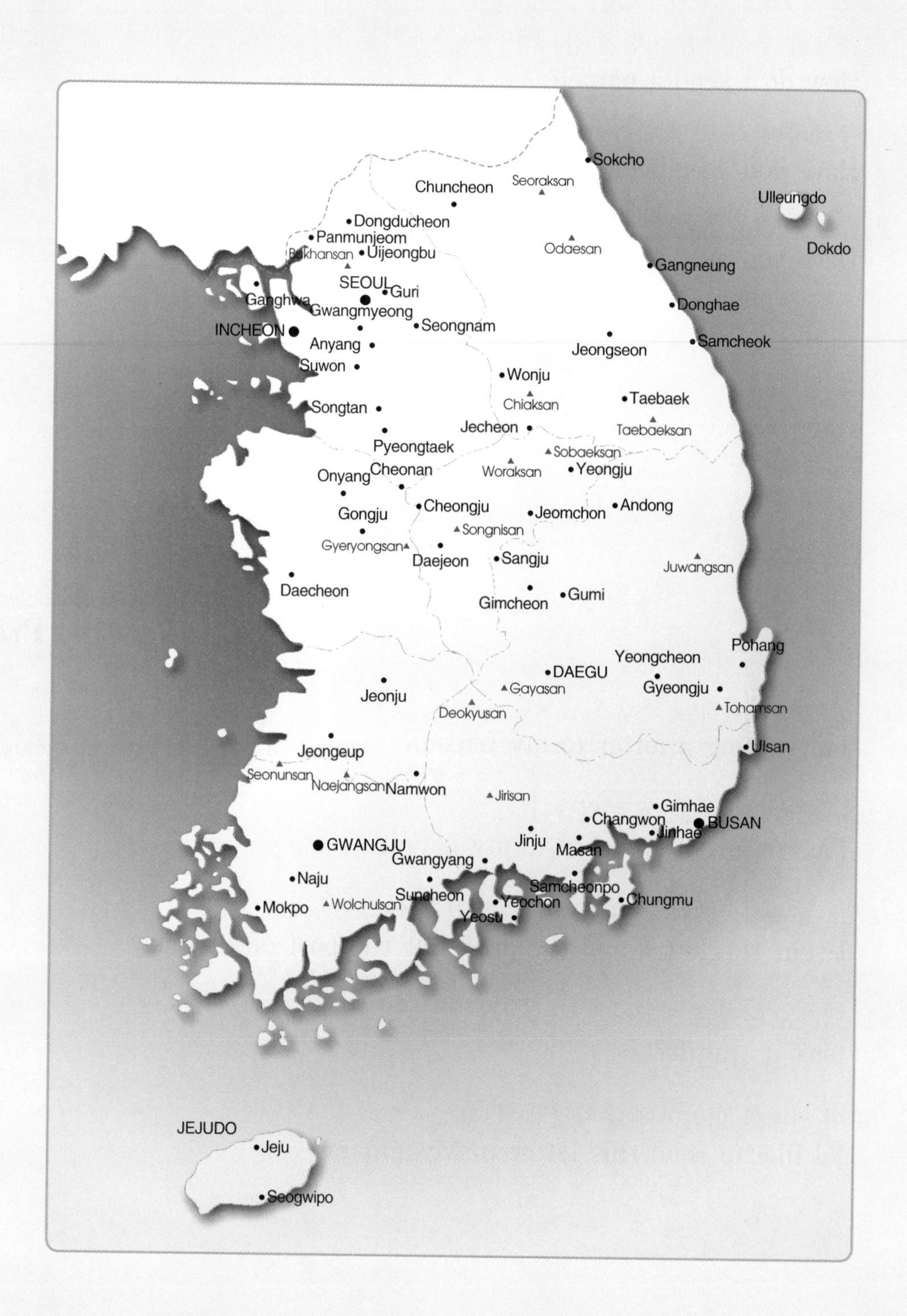
Sokcho
Chuncheon
Seoraksan
Ulleungdo
Dokdo
Dongducheon
Panmunjeom
Bukhansan
Uijeongbu
Odaesan
Gangneung
SEOUL
Guri
Ganghwa
Gwangmyeong
Donghae
INCHEON
Seongnam
Anyang
Jeongseon
Samcheok
Suwon
Wonju
Chiaksan
Taebaek
Songtan
Jecheon
Taebaeksan
Pyeongtaek
Sobaeksan
Onyang
Cheonan
Woraksan
Yeongju
Gongju
Cheongju
Jeomchon
Andong
Songnisan
Gyeryongsan
Daejeon
Sangju
Juwangsan
Daecheon
Gimcheon
Gumi
Pohang
Yeongcheon
DAEGU
Gyeongju
Gayasan
Jeonju
Deokyusan
Tohamsan
Ulsan
Jeongeup
Seonunsan
Naejangsan
Namwon
Jirisan
Gimhae
Changwon
BUSAN
Jinhae
GWANGJU
Jinju
Masan
Gwangyang
Naju
Samcheonpo
Suncheon
Chungmu
Mokpo
Wolchulsan
Yeochon
Yeosu
JEJUDO
Jeju
Seogwipo

Index

(국문 · 영문 · 불문 · 일문 색인)

ㄱ

국문	English	Français	日本語
가겠습니다 97	will go	J'arrive	行きます(意志)
가다 115	to go	aller	行く
가방 19	bag	le sac	カバン
가 보세요 67	please try to go...	aller voir	行って見てください
가 보시겠습니까? 73	Would (you) like to go and see...?	Voulez-vous me suivre, s'il vous plaît?	行ってご覧になってくださいませんか
가세요 13	to go/please go...	Vous allez ~	行く/行ってください
가세요? 67	(do you) go...?	allez-vous?	行くのですか
가야 되다 115	must go	il faut aller	行くべきだ, 行かなければならない
가을 25	fall(season)	l'automne	秋
가장 67	the most	le plus	一番
가져오다 37	to bring	apporter	持ってくる
가져오다/가져왔어요 26	to bring/brought	apporter/avoir apporté	持ってくる/持ってきました
가족 7	family	la famille	家族
가지 않겠습니까? 103	won't you go...?	ne voulez-vous pas aller à ...?	行きませんか
가지다 91	to have	avoir, passer	持つ
갈 거예요 67	will go	aller (futur)	行きます
갈 거예요? 31	will (you) go?	Allez-vous à ...?	行きますか
감사합니다 14	to thank	Je vous remercie.	ありがとうございます
갑니다 68	to go	aller	行きます
같이 109	with	avec, ensemble	一緒に
건물 109	building	le bâtiment	建物
걸려요 61	to take	falloir (concernant le temps)	かかります
걸리다 61	to take	prendre	かかる
검은색 86	black	noir	黒色
겨울 25	winter	l'hiver	冬
경주 67	Gyeongju (name of city)	Gyeongju	慶州
경주에 67	to Gyeongju	à Gyeongju	慶州に
계단 97	stairs	l'escalier	階段
계십니다 56	(one) is here	(Il/Elle) est là.	いらっしゃいます
계약 기간 74	terms of a contract	la durée du bail	契約期間
계약서 74	contract	le contrat	契約書
계절 25	season	la saison	季節
고마워요 37	to thank (polite informal)	merci	ありがとう
고맙습니다 13	to thank (polite formal)	Je vous remercie.	ありがとうございます
~고 싶다 93	want to	vouloir faire	(動詞語幹)たい
곧 98	soon	tout de suite	すぐ
공부 31	study	le travail	勉強
괜찮습니다 109	it's okay	non merci	大丈夫です
그 날 93	that day	ce jour-là	その日
그러면 19	then	alors	それでは
그런데 109	by the way	mais	しかし

그렇게 104	so	comme ça	そのように
그리고 50	and	et	そして
금방 98	soon	tout de suite	今すぐ
금요일 31	Friday	vendredi	金曜日
기다리다 79	to wait	attendre	待つ
기다리세요 49	please wait	Veuillez patienter un moment, s'il vous plaît.	待ってください
~까지 92	by	jusqu'à	~まで
깜짝 파티 92	a surprise party	la fête surprise	びっくりパーティー
깨끗하다 73	to be clean	propre	きれいだ
깨지다 116	to be fragile	être fragile	割れる
꼭 67	surely	sûrement	必ず
ㄴ			
나 2	I, me	Je, moi	私, 僕
나라 1	country	le pays	国
나아지다 98	to get better	aller mieux	良くなる
나아질 거라고 98	that (it) will get better	que ça ira mieux	良くなるだろうと
나이지리아 1	Nigeria	le Nigéria	ナイジェリア
나이키 86	Nike (Name of a brand)	Nike	ナイキ
날씨 25	weather	le temps	天気
남대문 시장 109	Namdaemun market	le marché Namdaemun	南大門 市場
남자 친구 38	male friends	un ami masculin (un copin)	ボーイフレンド
내리세요 61	please get off	descendez	お降りください
내리실 62	to get off	à descendre	お降りになる
내리실 문 62	exit	la porte de sortie	お降りになるドア
내일 31	tomorrow	demain	明日
넘어지다 97	to fall down	tomber	転ぶ, 倒れる
넣다 50	to put... in	mettre	入れる
누구 55	who	qui	誰
누구 찾으세요? 56	Who are you looking for?	Qui demandez-vous? (au téléphone)	誰をお探しですか
누르다 50	to push, to press	appuyer sur	押す
늦다 68	late	être en retard	遅い, 遅れる
ㄷ			
다섯 명 37	five people	cinq personnes	五名, 五人
다음 62	next	prochain	次
다음 역 62	next station	la prochaine station	次の驛
달다 116	measure	peser	量る
달아 보다 116	try to measure	essayer de peser	量ってみる
당신, 너 1	honorific 'you', nonhonorific 'you'	vous, tu	あなた, きみ
당신의 7	your	votre	あなたの
대한 슈퍼 14	Daehan supermarket	supermarché Daehan	大韓スーパー
더럽혀지다 109	to get dirty	être sale (se salir)	汚れる
덥다 26	to be hot	Il fait chaud.	暑い

~도 86	also	aussi	~も
도서관 31	library	la bibliothèque	圖書館
도시 67	city	la ville	都市
도와 주세요 97	please help (me)	Aidez-moi, s'il vous plaît. (Au secours)	助けてください
도장 79	signature stamp	la signature	はんこ
돈 75	money	l'argent	お金
돕다 97	to help	aider	助ける
동문 91	alumni	les anciens élèves d'une même école	同門, 同窓
동문들과 91	with alumni	avec les anciens élèves	同門たちと, 同窓生たちと
동문회 91	an alumni association	l'association d'anciens élèves	同門会, 同窓会
동생 7	younger brother or sister	le frère plus jeune	弟, 妹
동전 49	coin	des pièces de monnaie	硬貨
되세요 67	please become...	Bon (voyage).	なさいませ
두 명 38	two people	deux personnes	2人, 2名
두 시 55	two o'clock	2 heures	2時
드림 92	formality in writing letters (used after a name)	formalité à la fin d'une lettre	~より
드세요 98	please have(eat)...	mangez/prenez	召し上がってください
~드시겠습니까? 49	Would you like to have...?	Voulez-vous prendre ~?	召し上がりますか
들르다 92	to stop by	passer/ visiter	立ち寄る
따라가세요 62	please follow...	suivez	ついていってください
떠났어요 68	left	être parti	発ちました
~ㄹ 것 같아요 25	to seem	On dirait que...	~のようです ~だろう

ㅁ

마시다 50	to drink	boire	飲む
마시러 104	to drink	aller boire	飲みに
마실 것 104	something to drink	quelque chose à boire	飲み物
마실게요 50	(I will) drink...	(Je vais) prendre	飲みます
마십시오 98	please don't do...	ne pas faire	飲んでください
마음에 들어요 86	to be agreeable to one's mind	plaire à quelqu'un	気にいる
~만 111	only	mais	~だけ
만나다 1	to meet	se voir, rencontrer	会う
만날까요? 55	Shall (we) meet...?	Se voit-on?	会いますか?
만들다 81	to make	ouvrir (un compte courant)	作る
만들려고 81	to make	ouvrir (un compte courant)	作ろうと
많다 18	many	beaucoup	多い
많이 110	a lot, much	beaucoup	たくさん
말씀하다 97	to say, honorific	dire	おっしゃる
말씀해 주세요 97	please say...	(me)disez, s'il vous plaît	おっしゃってください
말하다 97	to speak	dire	言う, しゃべる
맛있다 49	to be delicious	délicieux	おいしい
매일 98	every day	chaque jour	毎日
맥도날드 55	McDonald's	McDonald's	マクドナルド
멋있다 109	to look good	chic	かっこいい

메뉴 49	menu	la carte	メニュー
몇 개 37	how many	combien de(chose)	いくつ
몇 명 37	how many people	combien de (personne)	何名, 何人
몇 시 55	what time	quelle heure	何時
모두 43	all	au total	みんな, 全部
모레 32	the day after tomorrow	après-demain	あさって
모르다 110	don't know	ne pas savoir	知らない, 分からない
모임 91	gathering /get together	la réunion	集まり, 会合
목걸이 19	necklace	le collier	ネックレス
무게 117	weight	le poids	重さ
무궁화호 67	Mugunghwaho(name of train)	Mugunghwaho	無窮花號
무슨(adj.) 103	what	quel	何
무슨, 무엇 31	what	quel	何
무엇 19	what	Qu'est-ce ~	なに
무엇을 7	what	Qu'est-ce ~	何を
무엇을 합니까? 7	What do (you) do?	Qu'est-ce que (vous faites)?	何をしますか
무엇입니까? 1	What is (it)?	Comment vous appelez-vous?	何ですか? 尋ねる
묻다 109	to stain	se tâcher	
물건 117	things, products	un objet	物
미얀마 2	Myanmar	Myanmar	ミャンマー
밀크 커피 50	coffee with milk	un café au lait	ミルクコーヒー

ㅂ

바나나 43	banana	une banane	バナナ
바라다 91	wish to, hope to	souhaiter	願う
바빠서 116	since it is busy	comme on est occupé	忙しくて
바쁘다 116	to be busy	être occupé	忙しい
바지 19	pants	le pantalon	ズボン
반갑습니다 1	to be nice to (meet you)	Ravi(e) de vous connaître	うれしいです
받을 사람 115	recipient	le destinataire	受取人
발 86	foot	le pied	足
방 73	room	une chambre	部屋
방금 68	soon	à l'instant	今さっき, たった今
배달하다 110	to deliver	livrer	配達する
배달해 드리다 110	to deliver	livrer	配達して差し上げる
배우다 7	to learn	apprendre	習う, 学ぶ
백 원짜리 49	a 100 won value	une pièce de 100 wons	100 ウォン玉
백 그램에 43	per 100g	pour 100g	100 グラムで
백화점 85	department store	le grand magasin	デパート
버튼 50	button	un bouton	ボタン
보고 싶어요 67	want to see	vouloir voir	会いたいです
보내는 사람 115	sender	l'expéditeur	差出人
보다 67	to see	voir	見る
보다/보았어요 26	to see/saw	voir / avoir vu	見る/見ました
보여요 13	to be seen	Vous-voyez ~?	見える

보증금 73	deposit	la caution	保証金
봉투 115	envelope	une enveloppe	封筒
부동산 75	real estate	l'immeuble	不動産
부디 91	please...	s'il vous plaît	ぜひ
부모님 115	parents	les parents	ご両親(両親)
부모님께 115	to parents	à (mes) parents	ご両親に
부쳐 주다 116	to send	envoyer	送ってくれる
부치다 115	to send	envoyer	送る
부탁하다 92	to ask	demander	頼む, 願う
불고기 49	Bulgogi	Bulgogi	焼き肉, プルゴギ
불국사 67	Bulguksa (name of a temple)	Bulguksa	仏国寺
붙이다 98	apply	appliquer	つける
블랙 커피 50	black coffee	un café noir	ブラックコーヒー
블럭 13	block	un bloc	ブロック
비 25	rain	la pluie	雨
비밀 100	secret	le secret	秘密
비밀 번호 80	PIN	le code secret / le code d'identification	秘密番号, 暗証番号
비빔밥 49	Bibimbap	Bibimbap	ビビンバップ, 混ぜご飯
빌려 주다/빌려 드리다 37	to lend	prêter	貸してくれる/貸してあげる
빌려 주세요 37	please lend me...	Prêtez-moi (chose)	

ㅅ

사호선 61	line 4 (subway)	la ligne 4	4號線
사다 85	to buy	acheter	買う
사람 1	person	l'homme	人
사려고 해요 85	try to buy	vouloir acheter	買おうとしています
사무실 74	office	bureau	事務室
사용하다 49	to use	utiliser	使用する, 使う
사이다 104	sprite (soda)	le soda	サイダー
사이즈 86	size	la pointure	サイズ
사자마자 109	as soon as I bought (it)	aussitôt que je (l')ai achetée	買ってすぐ
사천사백 원 43	4,400 won	4,400 wons	4,400ウォン
삼각지역 61	Samgakji station (a subway station)	la station Samgakji	三角地驛
삼, 사 일이면 98	in 3 or 4 days	dans 3 ou 4 jours	3, 4日なら
삼천칠백 원 44	3,700 won	3,700 wons	3,700ウォン
상표 86	brand	la marque	商標, マーク
새마을호 68	Saemaeulho (a kind of train)	Saemaeulho	セマウル號
색깔 86	color	la couleur	色
생각하다 98	to think	penser	考える, 思う
생일 31	birthday	le jour d'anniversaire (naissance)	誕生日
생일 파티 32	birthday party	la fête d'anniversaire	誕生パーティー
설렁탕 49	Seolleongtang (a Korean dish)	Seolleongtang	ソルロンタン(牛の骨のスープ)
설악산 68	Seorak Mountain	Mont Seorak	ソラクサン(雪岳山)

설탕 커피 50	coffee with sugar	un café sucré	砂糖入りコ-ヒ-
세 개에 43	for three	pour les trois	三つで
세 시 삼십 분 67	3:30	3heures 30	3時30分
세탁비 110	drycleaning fee	le tarif de blanchissage	洗濯費
세탁소 109	drycleaners	la blanchisserie	クリ-ニング屋
세탁하려고 110	to dryclean	pour faire un lavage	洗濯しようと
소개하다 7	to introduce	présenter	紹介する
소포 116	parcel	un colis	小包
손수건 116	handkerchief	un mouchoir	ハンカチ
쇼핑 103	shopping	le shopping	ショッピング
수영 103	swimming	la natation	水泳
수영하러 103	to swim	nager/ faire de la natation	水泳しに
수표 80	checks	un chèque	小切手
시간 91	time	le temps	時間
시간이 나다 92	to have time	avoir du temps/ être libre	暇がある, 時間がある
시원하다 25	to be cool	Il fait frais	涼しい
식사 후 98	after meal	après le repas	食事後
식사비 91	money for meal	la charge du repas	食費
신다 86	to wear	porter (pour les chaussures)	履く
신분증 79	an identification card	une pièce d'identité	身分証
신어 보다 87	try to wear	essayer de porter (pour les chaussures)	履いてみる
신청서 79	application form	une fiche de demande	申請書
실례합니다 13	excuse me	s'il vous plaît.	失礼します
싫어하다 104	to dislike	ne pas aimer/détester	嫌い
싫어해요 25	(I) dislike...	(Je) n'aime pas ～.	嫌いです
심한 98	severe	extrême/violent	ひどい
쓰고 있다 115	(I) am writing	être en train d'écrire	書いている, 使っている
쓰다 79	to write / to fill in	écrire	書く
씨 55	honorific suffix	Mme. / Mlle. / Mr.	~さん
～씨에게 91	to Mr. (Ms.) XX	Cher～/à	~さんに

ㅇ

아니다 2	no	ne pas être (ne pas venir de)	いいえ
아니오 2	no	non	いいえ
아닙니까? 116	isn't (it)...?	ce n'est pas～?	~ではありませんか
아닙니다 2	to be not	ne ... pas	~ではありません
아디다스 86	Addidas	Addidas	アディダス
아버지 7	father	le père	父, お父さん
아주 110	very	très	とても
아프다 97	to be sick	avoir mal	病いだ, (体の部位が)痛い
안 37	not	ne .... pas	~ない
안 계십니다 56	(he is) not here	(Il/Elle) n'est pas là	いらっしゃらない
안내원 85	information personnel	le personnel de l'accueil	案内員
안녕하세요? 1	hi	Bonjour	こんにちは(挨拶の言葉)
앉다 73	to sit	s'asseoir	座る
않다 103	not to do...	ne pas (faire)	~ない

알다 85	to know	connaître	知る, 分かる
알림 91	notice	l'annonce	お知らせ
앞면 115	front	en face	前面
약국 13	drugstore	la pharmacie	薬局
어느 1	which	quel	どの
어느 것 50	which one	lequel/laquelle	どれ
어느 정도 116	how long	combien de temps	どれぐらい
어느 쪽 62	which way	quelle direction	どちら, どっち
어디 13	where	où	どこ
어디에서 55	where	où	どこで
어떻게 49	how	comment	どうやって
어떻게 가요? 61	How (do I) get there?	Comment peut-on aller à ~?	どうやって行きますか
어떻습니까? 103	How is (it)?	comment ça va?	どうですか
어머니 7	mother	la mère	母, お母さん
어서 오세요 43	welcome	bienvenue	いらっしゃいませ
어제 31	yesterday	hier	昨日
언제 110	when	quand	いつ
언제, 언제예요? 31	when, When is (it)...?	quand, quand est-ce que ~ ?	いつ, いつですか
얼마입니까? 43	How much (does it cost)?	combien ça coûte?	いくらですか
얼마 정도 73	about how much	à peu près combien	いくらぐらい
없다 97	not	ne pas pouvoir	ない
없어요? 56	isn't there	ne pas être là?	ないですか
~에 31	in, at	à ~	~へ, ~に
~에서 31	in	à ~	~で, ~から
에스컬레이터 85	escalator	l'escalator	エスカレーター
엘리베이터 85	elevator	l'ascenseur	エレベーター
여권 번호 79	passport number	le numéro de passeport	パスポート番號
여기 37	here	ici	ここ
여기 있습니다 43	here it is	(le/la) voilà	ここにあります
여기 있어요 37	here it is	(le/la) voilà	ここにあります
여기에는 79	in here	ici	ここには
여보세요? 55	hello?	allô (au téléphone)	もしもし
여자 친구 38	female friends	une amie féminine (une copine)	ガールフレンド, 彼女
여행 67	trip	le voyage	旅行
연락 92	reply	la réponse	連絡
열차 68	train	le train	列車
옆 109	next	à côté	隣, 横
옆에 14	next to	à côté de	隣に, 横に
예 2	yes	oui	はい
예쁘다/예쁘군요 19	to be pretty	être joli	きれいだ/きれいですね
오월 31	May	mai	5月
오늘 25	today	aujourd'hui	今日
오다 32	to come	venir	来る
오다/오세요 32	to come/please come...	venir/venez	来る/来てください
오렌지 주스 104	orange juice	le jus d'orange	オレンジジュース
오른쪽 13	right side	à droite	右側

오백 원 62	500 won	500 wons	50ウォン
오이 43	cucumber	un concombre	きゅうり
오후 110	afternoon	l'après-midi	午後
올 것이다 92	will come	venir(futur)	来るでしょう
올림 91	formality attached after the sender's name in letters	formalité à la fin d'une lettre	~より
와/과 44	and	et	~と
와 주세요 92	please come...	Venez s'il vous plaît	来てください
왼쪽 14	left side	à gauche	左側
요즈음 116	these days	ces jours-ci	この頃
우리 32	we, us	nous	私たち
우리 ~해요 32	let's do...	faisons	私たち~しよう
우산 26	umbrella	le parapluie	傘
우체국 115	post office	la poste	郵便局
운동 98	exercise	l'exercice/ le sport	運動
운동화 19	sneakers	les chaussures de sport	運動靴
움직이다 97	to move	bouger	動く
월 73	month	mensuel, par mois	月
윗부분 115	upper part	en haut	上の部分
유명 67	famous	connu/célèbre	有名
유미 씨에게 92	to Yumi	à Yumi	ユミさんに
육 층 85	6th floor	le sixième étage	6階
음료수 104	beverage	la boisson	飲料水
～의 67	's (the possessive marker)	de	~の
의미 있는 91	meaningful	significatif	意味ある
이 49	this	ce(cette)	この
이 층 109	second floor	le deuxième étage	2階
이 킬로그램 43	2kg	2kg	2キログラム
이것은 19	this, it	ce	これは
이다 1	to be	être (venir de)	~だ
이다/입니다 19	to be	être ...	~だ, ~です
이런 109	oh-no! (exclamation)	Oh, non!	このような, こんな
이름 1	name	le nom	名前
이백육십 원 44	260 won	260 wons	260ウォン
이백이십 원 43	220 won	220 wons	220ウォン
이번 93	this time	cette fois	今度
이번 주 110	this week	cette semaine	今週
이십삼 일 31	23rd day	le 23	23日
이에요? 19	is this...?	Est-ce ...?	ですか
이제 104	now	maintenant	今, もう
이쪽 14	over here	par ici	こっち
이태원 55	Itaewon	Itaewon	梨泰院
인출 80	withdrawal	un retrait	引き出し
일 년으로 74	in one year	pour un an	1年で
일, 요일 31	day	jour	日, 曜日
일곱 시 32	seven o'clock	7 heures	7時
일기 예보 26	weather forecast	les prévisions météorologiques	天気予報

일반 상표 86	generic brand	les marques ordinaires	一般商標
일시 91	day and time	la date	日時
일시불 74	a lump sum payment	un paiement de somme forfaitaire	一括払い
일일구 구조대 97	119 rescue	les secours d'urgence le 119	119救助隊
잃어버렸어요 13	lost	avoir perdu	なくしました, 失いました
잃어버리다 13	to lose	perdre	なくす, 失う
~입니까? 19	is (it)...?	Qu'est ce que c'est? (Comment ça se dit...?)	~ですか
입다 110	to wear	porter	着る
있다 104	it is...	il y a	ある
있어요 13	it is...	il est	あります
있어요? 55	(where) is...?	être là?	ありますか

ㅈ

자동판매기 49	vending machine	un distributeur automatique	自動販売機
자취방 73	a self-boarding room	une chambre	自炊部屋
자판기 104	vending machine	un distributeur automatique	自動販売機
작성하다 73	to fill in	remplir	作成する
잘 104	well	bien	よく
잠깐 92	for a short time	pour un moment	しばらく, ちょっと
장소 91	place	le lieu	場所
재미있다 7	to be interesting	être intéressant	おもしろい
재킷 109	jacket	la veste	ジャケット
재학생 91	enrolled student	étudiants inscrits	在学生
저 103	I, me	Je, moi	私
저, 나 1	I, me	Je, moi	私/私の/僕
저것은 19	that	ça	あれは
저금하다 81	to save	épargner	貯金する
저기 13	over there	là-bas	あそこ
저기에 85	over there	là-bas	あそこに
저녁 32	evening	le soir	夕方, 夜, 夕ご飯
저예요 55	(it is) me	c'est moi (-même).	私です
저쪽 14	that way	par là	あちら
적다 8	not many	écrire	少ない
전통적인 67	traditional	traditionnel	傳統的な
전해 주세요 56	please tell...	Dites-lui que..., s'il vous plait.	傳えてください
전화 56	telephone	le téléphone	電話
전화 번호 97	phone number	le numéro de téléphone	電話番號
전화했다고 56	that I called	d'avoir téléphoné	電話したと
~정도 73	about, approximately	environ/à peu près	~くらい, ~ほど
정말로 104	really	vraiment	本当に
조금 68	a little	un peu	少し, ちょっと
존에게는 92	to John	à John	ジョンには
졸업생 91	graduate	l'ancien élève	卒業生
좋겠어요 38	will be good	Ce serait bien que	いいです

좋다 73	to be good	bon, agréable	良い
좋습니다 103	ok	d'accord	良いです
좋아하다 103	to like	aimer	好きだ
좋아하지 않지만 103	though I don't like...	je ne l'aime pas, mais	好きではないが
좋아합니다만 104	I like but...	je l'aime, mais	好きですが
좋아해요 25	to like	aimer	好きです
좋은 67	good	bon	良い
주다/주세요 8	to give/ please give...	donner/donnez-moi ~, s'il vous plaît.	くれる/ください
주말 103	weekend	le week-end	週末
주소 97	address	l'adresse	住所
주인 111	owner	le patron	主人
준비물 91	requirements(things for preparation)	les préparatifs	準備物
중간 부분 115	middle part	au milieu	中間部分
중국 116	China	la Chine	中国
지갑 13	wallet	le portefeuille	財布
지금 7	now	maintenant (actuellemeut)	今
지내다 91	to spend	aller	過ごす
지하철 61	subway	le métro	地下鉄
직업 7	occupation	le métier	職業
직접 116	in person	soi-même	直接
진통제 98	painkiller	le calmant	鎮痛剤
집 31	house	la maison	家
집 구경 73	taking a look at a house	visiter une chambre	家の下見
찜질약 98	medicated patch	la bande medicamenteuse	シップ薬

ㅊ

찾다 80	to withdraw	retirer	探す
찾다 85	to look for	chercher	探す
찾다 110	to get (it) back	récupérer	探す
찾으세요? 56	(who are you) looking for?	(Qui) demandez-vous?	探しますか
천백 원 43	1,100 won	1,100 wons	1,100ウォン
천천히 97	slowly	lentement	ゆっくり
초대장 92	invitation card	la carte d'invitation	招待状
춥다 25	to be cold	Il fait froid	寒い
치마 20	skirt	la jupe	スカート
친구 8	friend	un ami	友だち
친목 91	getting together	faire des amis	親睦

ㅋ

커피 104	coffee	le café	コーヒー
콜라 104	cola	le coca	コーラ

ㅌ

타세요 61	please take	prendre	乗ってください
태평양 대학교 7	Taepyeongyang University	Université Taepyeongyang	太平洋大学

FIRST STEP IN KOREAN

1999년 3월 25일 초판 발행
2018년 11월 30일 초판 제17쇄 발행

原著者 慶熙大學校 平生敎育院
代表著者 李 淑 子
發行者 金 哲 煥
發行處 民衆書林

10881 경기도 파주시 회동길 37-29
(파주출판문화정보산업단지)
전화 (영업) 031) 955-6500~6 (편집) 031) 955-6507
Fax (영업) 031) 955-6525 (편집) 031) 955-6527
홈페이지 http: // www.minjungdic.co.kr
등록 1979. 7. 23. 제2-61호

정가 13,000원

ISBN 978-89-387-0041-4 13710

택시 61	taxi	un taxi	タクシ-
택시로 61	by taxi	en taxi	タクシ-で
테니스 103	tennis	le tennis	テニス
토마토 43	tomato	une tomate	トマト
토요일 110	Saturday	le samedi	土曜日
통장 80	bank book	un livret de banque	通帳
티셔츠 116	T-shirt	unT-shirt	Tシャツ

ㅍ

파란색 37	blue	bleu	青色
파출소 13	police station	le poste de police	派出所
펜 37	pen	un stylo	ボ-ルペン
편지 115	letter	une lettre	手紙
표 68	ticket	billet	切符, チケット
표시 62	sign	le panneau	しるし
프로스펙스 86	Prospecs (name of a brand)	Prospecs	プロスペクス

ㅎ

하고 있다 115	be doing	être en train de	~している
하다 98	to do	faire	する
하지만 92	but	mais	けれども
학교 31	school	l'école	学校
한 13	one	un	一, 一つ
한 번 86	one time	une fois	一回
한 장 67	one	un (billet)	一枚
한국 67	Korea	la Corée	韓国
한국어 7	The Korean language	le coréen(langue)	韓国語
한국어로 19	in Korean	en coréen	韓国語で
한국어반 91	Korean language class	classe de coréen	韓国語クラス
한국인 8	Korean	le coréen(la personne)	韓国人
할 수 있어요? 73	can (you) do?	Puis-je?	できますか
합시다 74	let's do...	faisons	しましょう
해 주다 92	to do	rendre service/donner	してくれる
현금 80	cash	l'argent liquide	現金
헤어지다 56	to say goodbye	pour dire au revoir	別れる
현금 카드 80	cash card	une carte bancaire	現金カ-ド
형 7	elder brother	le frère aîné	お兄さん, 兄
혼자 109	alone	seul	一人
화장실 13	restroom	les toilettes	トイレ
확인하다 81	to confirm	vérifier/confirmer	確認する
확인해 보다 81	try to confirm	essayer de vérifier	確認してみる
회사원 7	office worker	l'employé de bureau dans une société	会社員
~후 98	after	après	~後
흐리다 25	to be cloudy	Il fait nuageux	曇る
흰색 86	white	blanc	白色

FIRST STEP IN KOREAN

외국인을 위한
한국어 입문 시리즈

한국어를 쉽고 빠르게 익힐 수 있는 지름길!

경희대 이숙자 교수

FIRST STEP IN KOREAN / 외국인을 위한 한국어 입문

FIRST STEP IN KOREAN FOR CHINESE / 중국인을 위한 한국어 입문

FIRST STEP IN KOREAN FOR FRENCH / 프랑스인을 위한 한국어 입문

FIRST STEP IN KOREAN FOR JAPANESE / 일본인을 위한 한국어 입문

FIRST STEP IN KOREAN FOR RUSSIAN / 러시아인을 위한 한국어 입문

FIRST STEP IN KOREAN FOR SPANISH / 스페인인을 위한 한국어 입문

EXPLORING KOREAN / 외국인을 위한 한국어 읽기